How I Found Myself In Egypt

How I Found Myself In Egypt

Mecca Jihad

Library of Congress Control Number: 2013916574

This book was printed in the United States of America.

Editor: Halimah Ceesay
desertfountain7@aol.com

ISBN:	Softcover	978-1-4797-9405-8
	Ebook	978-1-4797-9406-5

Printed in the United States of America by BookMasters, Inc
Ashland OH
Apr 2014

Rev. date: 10/11/2013

To order additional copies of this book, contact:
Xlibris LLC
1-888-795-4274
www.Xlibris.com
Orders@Xlibris.com
130664

Chapter 1

In the name of Allah, the Most Beneficent, the Most Merciful

> **"See they not that they are tried once or twice every year (with different kinds of calamities, disease, famine, etc.)? Yet they turn not in repentance, nor do they learn a lesson." (Quran 9:126)**

The eyes of students were glued to the TV, watching as the plane went crashing into the World Trade Center. I watched too but with stilled emotion, not realizing the magnitude of what had taken place. I'm sure it was an accident, I thought to myself and casually went about my day. It wasn't until it was reported that Osama Bin Laden claimed responsibility and Muslims were attacked that I came down from my innocent little cloud and realized the implications of what had taken place.

I had been on my way to a morning class at Medgar Ever College when it was announced that courses for the rest of the day were cancelled, so I decided to go the Mosque as I usually did between classes. When the crowd of people waiting for the bus steadily increased without there being any bus in sight, I knew something was wrong. I left the ever-hopeful people at the bus stop and began to walk the 15 minute hike as I did on occasion. It wasn't until I reached closer to my destination in the Bedford Stuyvesant neighborhood that I came in contact with more pedestrians; it was a moment that changed my life forever.

I struggled to unwrap myself from my mother's warm quilt and tried ever so hard to motivate myself to get out of bed and get ready. Just the thought of what could be waiting out there for me once I stepped out of the door, frightened me. With no one to accompany me to school, I had better be ready to brave what I would face.

I was dressed in a flowery, navy blue skirt that covered my ankles, a long sleeve shirt and a blue hijab on my head, pinned at the neck and draped over my chest. I could have easily blended in with the society if I wanted to, without any worry of being attacked. During that time my brown face would have not stricken an offence, since it was lynching season for the Muslims and Arabs. But as scary it was, knowing that my Islamic garb made me a moving target, I could *not* remove my hijab. The firm Islamic principles imbedded in me by my parents, made me stand firm even in my feebleness. I said Bismillah, offered dua and proceeded to the bus station around the corner, where my hour-and-half commute on public transportation from Jamaica, Queens to Brooklyn would begin. There was no turning back.

"Religion is a bunch of rituals!" said the Psychology Professor. Did I just hear him right? Shock inhibited my speech. I was appalled that he would make such a bias comment. By the time I recovered, the professor had already moved on to another topic. Besides the missed opportunity, I was not in a position to challenge the professor, or anyone for that matter. Trepidation was intensified and left me feeling vulnerable like never before.

The topic of Islam would randomly come up in classes and I had to be ready. I prepared myself for the animosity, rage and hate. People would repeat misconceptions about Islam, putting the pressure on me, as the only Muslim in the class to correct them. I wasn't prepared for this at all. I had a hard time speaking up in public as it was and now I had *more* of a reason to be nervous. I was shaken like never before.

"I don't understand that religion!" one of my Professors said to me in a conversation we had only a couple of days after the catastrophic incident. I had regarded him as someone positive and open minded and never imagined such words coming out of his mouth. Based on what was presented in the media, he had already made an assessment about a religion practiced by over a billion people worldwide. It is calamitous how many people can do so without taking the time to open the Qur'an, a compilation of Hadiths or even attempting to study Islam. Since we were talking one-on-one, I felt comfortable speaking up. I confidently challenged him and left him with something to think about. Alhumdulillah, we were able to wrap up the discussion on a positive note.

However, it didn't go as smoothly with my Psychology Professor. He was a bitter, old man who had a long line of students who often complained about him. It was said that this white man enjoyed working at a predominately Black school, so that he could derail, discourage and dissuade as many students as he could. I soon learned that his prejudice extended into the realm of Islam, and me fitting both his disgusts, caused me to suffer extensively from the brunt from his abhorrence.

My inability to respond to his contempt encouraged him to provoke me even more. I tried to put on a valiant face but any moment I felt like I was going to break from the pressure. The Psychology Professor went out of his way to make me feel discomfort; to say that he took delight in seeing me squirm was an understatement. I wished I could hide my coyness and play cool, but no matter how much I tried, I couldn't. I was disappointed in myself. Why couldn't I just go in there, stare the Professor in the face, take notes and refrain from shivering from his disdain?

I kept my mouth shut and tried to avoid conflict, except on one occasion. It was right after 9/11 in my Psychology class, when discussion was centered on the domestic security breach. One of my peers appeared to parrot what she heard as opposed to analyzing the facts to come up with her own conclusion. To my own surprise, I spoke up. I challenged the validity of her argument.

As a journalist-in-training, I knew the importance of sources being verified. However, I understood that it's much easier to take what is presented before you than to collect and discern information objectively. Whether the information is presented by a news broadcaster or in print, I didn't forget that people behind the news are *not* infallible. Otherwise, there wouldn't be a constant revolving door of retractions made each year.

It was only natural that I would study journalism in college; I have always been an inquisitive person, asking 101 questions, even if it's just to myself, to make sense of things. I was no lawyer and no expert but I know that it may take weeks or months before evidence is discovered, analyzed and a detailed investigation in launched before a crime is solved.

Moments after the plane hit the WTC, it was being reported that Osama Bin Laden and "his followers" were cited as responsible for the crime. The people were angry and someone had to pay.

If you were dressed in a certain way, you were a target, which explains why not only Muslims were being attacked but Hindus and Sikhs as well an any other who were mistaken as Muslims.

The student I questioned was defensive. I expected this. She responded to my disparagement with more things that she heard. "They said . . . ," she testified as if no one could tell her anything different. I don't even know why I bothered to say anything, I thought to myself. I felt like giving up but knew that I couldn't.

Unfortunately before 9/11 I didn't have the practice of soothing my soul by reading the Quran and making constant thikr of Allah, so trying to pick it up now was nearly impossible; I could barely make it through the day. Also, being that I hadn't experienced my problems melting away while reciting the Glorious words of Allah in the original language, I didn't realize how much I was losing by not being able to take shelter in these life-saving rituals during these trying times.

And since I failed to seize the opportunity to really invest in the cultivation of my spirit like I should have, I lost out. I gave some time to these practices but not the same effort and hard work that I gave to other things, things that produced more immediate results like a good grade on a report card or money. I would learn the results of neglecting the spirit to be pricier than losing all of your property and wealth; if you don't check yourself; you are in danger of becoming bankrupt.

Devoting the necessary time and attention to my courses was another struggle. I wasn't able to really focus during class or open up the book outside of class. My mind wondered to my safety and welfare and that of my family and the Muslims in general.

I never felt ever so physically weak and mentally drained. The unsettling atmosphere kept me on edge. My soul felt weighed down by the murky cloud of danger. But that was just the beginning.

I felt butterflies in my stomach. Something told me to expect *something* from the Psychology Professor. The topic in my Psychology class was related to jealousy, the feeling that usually comes over a child when their new sibling comes on the scene; they resent sharing toys with them and may start to act out now that someone new has stolen attention from them.

The hands on the clock didn't move fast enough for me. I was on edge, unable to relax, anticipating an unruly comment from the Professor until I paused for a moment to reflect. In the entire class, the Professor actually refrained from saying anything disrespectful or crude. As a matter of fact, during the last previous classes he spared me his derision and said nothing relating to religion at all. Maybe, he had finally put it to rest, I hoped inwardly. But while wrapping up the session, he made his mark by topping off all the insults ever made in class; he uttered the most outlandish, uncalled for statement that would forever jog my memory.

" . . . when your husband comes home and says I want another wife," he said haughtily, tying in the topic of jealousy to a hypothetical situation where a Muslim woman may learn about her husband's interest in practicing polygamy.

The Professor sat back in his seat and gave me one of those sadistic smiles. The class was over and I was left frozen in disbelief. The comment caused me to immediately cease packing my bag and began to turn the wheels in my head, in search of a rebuttal, a resolution or anything at all. My mind frantically tried to come up with something but it was still stumped from the undermined attack.

I was lost for words and found it difficult to even report him as he was the chair of the Psychology Department. Even if I complained to the President of the school, with no proof, it'll just me my word against his.

The sound of the college students instigating rung in my ears, making me feel even more disrespected. There was a synchronized melody of students saying "oooohhh!" like the little kids did when one of their peers silenced another in a joking match. Not only was the professor calling me out but the entire class bore witness to it.

It didn't take a Psychologist to see what he was doing: the crude comments, looking me up and down and giving me dirty looks while I entered the class and doing and saying things to direct my attention. It was clear that he was trying to push my buttons but I wasn't going to give him any satisfaction by reacting. I continued to smile and be respectful to him as I did with all my Professors. Instead of responding to his ignorance, I chose to follow the example of Prophet Muhammad, peace and Blessings be upon him, whose character was a walking Qur'an.

Chapter 2

"O you who believe! If a Fâsiq (liar—evil person) comes to you with any news, verify it, lest you should harm people in ignorance, and afterwards you become regretful for what you have done." (Quran 49:6)

The misinformation being fed to the masses about Islam was overwhelming. So many untruths were bluntly being written about Islam and the people digested it with little questioning. This was dangerous. There were people who thought Jihad meant holy war and only Allah knows how many people thought that the people who committed the horrendous act were martyrs. Some of the concepts in Islam were either distorted; other times, plain old lies were relayed. I held the writers fully responsible for what their hands sent forth, for they are professionals who should be fully aware of their responsibility to deliver the truth. In addition, I faulted the Muslims for being so passive. We should be abreast of what is being written about Islam and take action immediately when we are being misrepresented. Now, after allowing such lies to spread for so long can we really get mad when people begin to believe them? When the misinformation is even more damaging after a catastrophic event like 9/11, we have to devote double the effort, sacrifice triple the time, and invest in quadruple as many resources to convert the losses into wins.

The fight was too great for me to think that I could do it alone. I was not equipped to challenge every student or even attempt to battle every prejudiced professor. I asked about the Muslim Student Association. To me, I didn't think we had a choice in the matter. As Muslims we have an obligation to give dowah and the MSA was a beneficial tool to do just that; dispel the myths and misconceptions, promote and encourage dialogue between Muslims and Non Muslims on campus and open the floor for information sessions, lectures and the like. If anything, this was the time for Muslim students everywhere to make sure there was an active MSA at their school.

The MSA at my school was vacant and I was on a mission to get it revamped. After searching for Muslims on campus, I finally found a Muslim brother who was able to give me some information; he said that the MSA has been in defunct for some time, which means when it was time for other club activities, the Muslims couldn't be found. This was embarrassing, to say the least.

I went to the Student Government Office to investigate. They showed me a huge bag full of unclaimed mail.

"It's a shame because the MSA gets more mail than any other club," I was told.

I asked what I had to do to get the club up and running again. I wasn't seeking to be leader but the club needed to be lead and no one was stepping up to the plate; in order to get the club rolling again the President needed to be present, so I intended to fulfill that role. Alhumdulillah, before you knew it, I ran into a few Muslims on campus and encouraged them to be involved. Allah blessed us to be successful in getting the club recognized again, which authorized us to meet and conduct activities like every other club. I also found the last president who had been missing in action. I didn't bother questioning him about the MSA being vacant for so long. I simply told him that we would commence with the meetings and I was taking over now. He didn't show any resistance or much concern at all.

We established the offices. I was the president and the former President, Abdul Salam, was the Vice President. Soon after, the positions of secretary and treasurer were filled. I rushed to establish this for the facilitation of the paperwork and for the overall function of the club without reviewing the responsibility of each office and making sure the people was qualified for their role. Later on I would learn that this was a huge mistake. My main concern was getting the club up and running but I overlooked the importance of the members doing their part and working as a team. This was even more significant than getting the paperwork straight, because if the foundation isn't steady, it doesn't matter what you put on paper, the club won't survive.

Nevertheless, I was very pleased with the progress we made. We had a prominent Imam give a lecture on Jihad; he broke down what it actually meant and left the attendees with a clear understanding of what it was. One student exclaimed how happy she was now that she learned the truth about Islam and the real meaning of Jihad. How many people out there are still in the dark?

I arrived bright and early, ready to start my new internship. I was amazed how it happened. A mere converse with someone was paramount in a major shift taking place in my life. It's amazing how Allah does things!

I stepped into the weekly newspaper establishment, smiling and warmly greeting the people. It didn't take long for me to realize that I wasn't welcomed. I was the only African American in the office and judging by the way they treated me, maybe even the first Muslim they've ever come in contact with.

People stared at me and gave me disapproving looks. I attempted to build a rapport with my new co-workers but many of them avoided eye contact with me as all costs and chose to pass by me as if I didn't exist. I grew immune to it; I was neither hurt nor disappointed. It was expected, though very sad, given the heavy duty of journalists to be objective and fair. How can one be objective in their writing if they fail to even acknowledge their preconceived notions? Here I was, merely a journalist-in-training and I appeared to be more open-minded than my professional colleagues who were hold in such high esteem by the public.

I wasn't going to allow their petty behavior to change me. Though it was quite discouraging to have my cheerily smiles countered with frowns and malice, I made the decision to remain upbeat and outgoing. It wasn't about them; I didn't feel right passing by them without saying anything, even if I knew they were going to ignore me.

I knew they were intimidated and fearful of what they didn't know, which is why I didn't feed into their pessimism. I wanted to show them there was nothing to be fear. I understood that they didn't know much about Islam but the fact of the matter is, unless they are willing to come out of their box, they will continue to remain ignorant.

I was grateful everyone wasn't sour. The managing editor, the one who hired me, was very friendly and kind-spirited. His warmth made up for all of the acrimony I ever felt in that office. It was a blessing too because he was the one who would supervise and evaluate me. Could you imagine if I had to report to someone who abhorred me? It would have been very challenging for me to make any progress. But out of infinite mercy from Allah, he blessed me with a down—to—earth editor, who treated me with nothing but respect. Which of the favors of your Lord do you deny?

Chapter 3

"The forgiver of sin, the Acceptor of repentance, the Severe in punishment, the Bestower (of favors). None has to be worshipped but He. To Him is the final return." (Qur'an: 40:3)

I paused when the editor-in-chief of the school newspaper asked me my opinion about homosexuality. This was something that despite my efforts to avoid pondering about, stayed on my subconscious mind the majority of the time.

I turned to the Scriptures to see what God said about homosexuality. In the Qur'an, Allah tells us what happens to the people who came before who practiced sodomy. They were given chance after chance but when they insisted on sinning, without repenting, they were hit with something catastrophic that would terribly shake them like never before.

I knew the editor-in-chief of the school newspaper was testing me. She witnessed my ability to be objective, unbiased and conduct myself in a professional manner but she also knew that I was religious. She caught me off guard. I was still deciding how I would approach the topic of homosexuality while practicing journalism and wasn't quite sure if it was possible. Would I be able to show a strong opposition to this sin and still maintain a credible reputation as an objective journalist or would I have to adopt a mild attitude towards it if my profession calls for it?

Though I have a right to an opinion, just as anyone else, I've learned if you have the backing of the "right people," it won't be held against you. In the age where people are threatened from losing their jobs if they say anything disapproving against homosexuality, I knew I had to play my cards right me. Someone else may be able to get away with exercising their first amendment right, but I had to be careful; I knew anything I did and said would be held against me. I didn't want to jeopardize any chances of me advancing my career; I wanted to at least get my foot in the door.

The editor-in-chief looked at me in my eyes waiting for my response. I avoided answering the question and re-directed the conversation to the problem of rape in the prison system. I relayed to her my genuine concern of inmates being scared and psychologically bruised for a lifetime and in many cases, altering their lifestyles. It is my belief that all of them don't make a conscious decision to become homosexuals or bisexuals but after an experience like that, without getting therapy and coming to terms with what happened with them, some of them do change their sexual preference. Though some may feel conflicted, in today's pro-homosexuality world, instead of being encouraged to deal with their issues and seek help, they may not just chuck it up to life being hard and end up pushing their hitches under the rug instead of acknowledging what happened to them and seeking healing.

I was not up-playing my concern for inmates; I was truly bothered by anyone being abused, treated as guinea pigs or being taken advantage of, regardless of who they were. It's not right for any human being to be mistreated, whether they are inmates or not.

The Muslim Student Association had officially been dismembered and rendered inactive again. Hajar, Abdul Salam and Yah Yah weren't able to get it together. After having many arguments with Abdul Salam, and attempting to move forward with the club, Hajar finally gave up and the drive that Abdul Salam had at the end of my term to "stay on top of things" suddenly disappeared. He went back to his previous practice of not showing up for meetings. The Vice President stopped attending meetings as well and on many occasions Hajar was the only one there waiting; she walked away disgruntled, vowing not to bother with the MSA again.

"You look so beautiful!" one of the female employees from the newspaper said to me. I couldn't believe my ears. This woman was probably the one who was most adamant in ignoring me, screwing up her face at me and making me feel like I didn't belong. Not once did she respond to my greetings or acknowledge my presence. Now here she was complementing me on my dress! I could hardly believe it. She sounded so sincere, like she was admiring my dress and couldn't help but to express herself. Before you knew it, she was asking me the proper name for my headdress and we had established a rapport. I would have never predicted this in a million years. I had just accepted people for being who they are and in the process of being affable, something made this woman approach me. After speaking with her that day, there wasn't a day that passed that we didn't converse. Even among her other colleagues, she still talked to me naturally, without any hesitation or embarrassment. I respected her for doing what most people won't allow themselves to do: let go of fear and attempt to visit time outside your comfort zone; you just may be pleasantly surprised.

There were a few other pleasant and respectful people from the newspaper establishment who I conversed with from time to time. Prior to this, I haven't had much interaction with Whites; my experience of entering the "White World" for the first time. All the schools I attended were populated by Muslims, until I attended Junior High School; attending public schools for the first time was an automatic exchange from Muslim students to mainly Black ones. I interacted with a few people here and there but to me it wasn't a big deal.

I never shied away from being around White people. As a matter of fact, when it came to attending colleges, I considered attending Anglo Saxon Schools, but I came to thank Allah for placing me at Medgar Evers College; surely, Allah is the best of planners.

Though this was one of my few times interacting with White people, it really wasn't a big deal to me. I never felt intimidated being among them nor did I feel a need to prove myself worthy of being in their presence. Some Black folks find themselves working or living among Whites, and began to think too much of themselves. I knew better than that. Just because I happened to work among whites, that didn't make me any more special than I already was. The true criterion for determining superiority is our hearts, our deeds and our reverence for our Creator, not the color of our skins. As a matter of fact, even our skin color is determined by God, so how can we take credit for that? How dare we attempt to rank people and set a value on them based on the color of their skin? Ranking people is Allah's job and anyone who attempts to take it on will *never* be qualified to do so.

I was starting to feel sick to my stomach attending the internship. I was surrounded by toxic people who got a kick out of cursing, complaining and backbiting. I spent wishing that perhaps my spirit would be spared from their abuse. I wished I could wear a pair of headphones and tune out everything they had to say but I couldn't do so because I had to be alert to the happenings and communicate with them. I could tolerate people ignoring me and making me feel unwelcome but this other stuff was killing my spirit. I sat in the back area, literally surrounded by three individuals who couldn't help their distasteful behavior. They talked about their co-workers ferociously yet met them with smiles and pleasant conversation. If this is what they did to their White counterparts, what could *I* expect from them?

They smiled at me, responded when I wished them a good morning and even struck up conversation with me from time to time. I was friendly with them but there was a limit to how much I would allow myself to be around them. I made small talk with them but kept it professional. I didn't eat with them or engage in any activity with them outside of work. I understood the mentalities that I was dealing with so I had to do what I had to in order to prevent as much contamination as possible. I continued to pray and looked forward to the day my internship was over.

The managing editor couldn't stop complementing me on the first article that I wrote. I was embarrassed by how much he praised me. To me, I didn't have any other choice but to do my best. In fact, being that I didn't expect to get recognition made me more focused on the mission at hand. Therefore, whether I got praise or not, it didn't matter to me; not receiving praise would *not* disappoint me and receiving praise would *not* get to my head. The article made it into the newspaper, without hardly any edits being made, if any at all. I was developing into the craftier journalist that I dreamed of becoming. Allah is so Akbar!

"I want you to leave your work and come with us. We're taking you to lunch!"

I looked up from my computer. It was the managing editor. I could hardly believe my ears. It was my last day interning and he surprised me by treating me to a restaurant in the area! My heart melted. They thought enough about me to treat me to lunch! I was so grateful for what Allah had done for me and what he was saving for me. I looked back to my days of searching endlessly for an internship and was getting roadblocks. He appointed for the freshman to tell me about the newspaper and secured for me a place there at the perfect time. Not only that but he finally used me as a vessel that would open up the hearts and minds of individuals at the establishment and have a lasting impression on them. I was taken back at the way Allah made everything happen. We can *never* predict the way God works but we can rest assured that in the end, everything will work out just fine.

The "original members" of the MSA were nowhere to be found and the MSA was immobile for a full semester. I waited and watched to see if anyone would take action but nothing happened. A part of me wanted to walk away but my conscious wouldn't let me rest. I went back to the SGA and did the similar process that I did in the beginning to get the MSA rolling again. But this time instead of giving myself the responsibility of leadership, I reached out to the new batch of Muslims enrolled in the University and relayed to the importance of the MSA being re-established; they seemed to be motivated and agreed to attend the first meeting. Alhumdulillah, though we had been defunct, our privileges for using the room, designated for the club, wasn't taken away from us. I wanted to be involved in the club but I realized the wisest thing was for me to take a back seat. I was on my way out of the school and I needed to remain focused. I decided to provide the support and advisement from a distance until things were established. It was a rocky start but Alhumdulillah, AFTER DIFFICULTY COMES EASE! The brother who rarely attended meetings due to his extremely busy schedule, not only came back to the club but he assumed responsibility as president. He did a wonderful job and never showed any negligence in the least. I couldn't be happier.

Chapter 4

Why should Allah punish you if you have thanked Him and believed in Him. And Allah is All Appreciative (of good), All knowing." (Qur'an 4:147)

After all the pain, sweat and tears, the time for me to graduate finally arrived! I walked across the stage and exhaled, knowing that I would be able to benefit from the seeds that I sowed. I didn't have a job right after graduating but I wasn't worried; I afforded myself the time to rejuvenate and take a breather before getting back out there and continuing my job search. I had a job offer on the table from the newspaper where I interned; it was mine for the taking but I declined. The environment would have polluted me; my insides were already suffering being around those toxic individuals just one day a week; imagine if I worked with them five days a week. I considered it, at least until I got something better but I couldn't do it; I wasn't going to oppress my spirit even further. It's one thing if I didn't have a choice but I have options, I reminded myself. I don't care if it takes me a couple of months before I find something; it's better to be patient and find some place suitable, than to settle and regret it later on.

After sending out my resume and going on a couple of interviews, Allah blessed me to find something, but it wasn't a job that I applied for; it was a blessing that God dropped in my lap, from different avenue; He was pulling me in another direction, little did I know it.

One of the faculty members from my College invited me to work at her non-profit organization, the Center for Black Literature. The position was Program Coordinator. Since I interned there, while in college, I had a taste of what I would be doing had I decided to take up employment there.

I was honored she thought enough of me to work there. Though it wasn't in the journalism field, I sensed it would be worth my time and attention to join this reputable organization.

I was the person behind the scenes to make sure that everything ran smoothly; I dealt with the administrative side, pulling strings, helping to organize events, following up with matters and trouble shooting. I got to work early in the morning and often times returned home late. I worked on the weekends when functions were held and assisted in setting up and filling in whenever the help was needed. Though I wasn't always compensated monetarily for the extra time and work, the experience was a reward in itself, not to mention the sense of accomplishment I felt after seeing how nicely everything came together. What impressed me the most were the programs put together for the inner-city youth in the community. A curriculum was constructed to implement a creative writing course, thereby giving the students an outlet to express themselves and have a sense of accomplishment by showcasing their work at the end of the program. There was nothing like witnessing the work produced by the students. It made me so proud of all the teachers, artists and other individuals who came together and worked so beautifully to cultivate these youngsters and bring about such a wonderful performance at the end of the program.

On one occasion, the extraordinary revolutionary, Sonia Sanchez was invited to speak to a group of students from a local high school. I attended early to set up and do my duty, not realizing the magnitude of the event. Though the program was for the students, *I* was left feeling empowered, invigorated and rejuvenated. Not only did Sonia Sanchez's genuine talk shape the youngsters but it affected the adults too. Moments like these made all the extra hours and time exerted worth it. It helped me to stay focus and maintain gratitude. We may not always get compensated for our work but should we stop, knowing the work has to get done?

Meeting Sonia Sanchez in person and hearing her speak was priceless. Working at the Center has allowed me to realize the value of bringing about change-provoking events like this one. It was an honor to be a part of a revolutionary change, to the reach out and touch the lives of those who are often ignored and struggling to find something to live for. Stimulating minds stimulated me and I was so grateful to take part in this most revered act! The Center for Black Literature put on conferences, functions and events where thought-provoking ideas were shared, debated and considered. People were able to hear from the less popular writers, some who may be censored or downplayed to those were more popular. I was appreciative for the privilege I had of being exposed to some of the most brilliant and gutsy writers, most of whom I probably would have never heard of had I remained austerely committed to the mainstream literary medium.

After working at the Center for Black Literature for about a year, I was extremely grateful for reaching such an astonishing milestone and was ready to graduate to the next stage. No doubt, it was an incredible experience working there but deep down inside I yearned to do more.

The editor-in-chief of my school newspaper sent an e-mail to undisclosed recipients informing us about a job opening a daily newspaper where she worked. It was a part-time, administrative assistant position that she held. She was hoping to find a suitable replacement for her as she was on her way out. I thought it would be a great opportunity for me to get back into the journalism field so I displayed interest in the position. She told me that she'd get back to me. I knew something wasn't right after a few weeks passed and I still hadn't heard from her. Instead of waiting for her to respond to my e-mail, I called her and she informed me that she spoke to her boss about me. Great! I thought to myself, until I discovered exactly what she said to her. I was shocked when I learned what she said.

"I told my boss I know someone but the only problem is she's Muslim," the former editor-in-chief said to me.

I had to take a moment to compose myself. Did I just hear my colleague right? Someone who knew me, who could vouch for my tenacity and great journalistic skills, someone who knew I was beyond qualified for the job was presenting the possibility of me working there as a problem simply because of my choice of faith. I never saw my religion as a problem but apparently in her eyes, there was an issue.

"I don't know if you'll be willing to take off your burka, what do you call it?" she continued. I was insulted. Not only is it a problem for me to be Muslim but I should be the one to give up my first amendment right and abandon my commitment to this life-long practice of covering my hair in order to be socially accepted and allowed to work someplace.

"It's a hijab and no, I'm not willing to take it off," I responded with poise.

I was able to mask my emotion while listening to her explanation. I felt disappointment and sadness well up inside of me, as the rising emergence of anger threatened to take over. I was disappointed in her action of forewarning her boss, sad that my work ethic wasn't good enough to get a job that I was suitable for and angry knowing things like this happen all the time; people are discriminated against and denied opportunity before they even have a chance to get out there and show that they are just as good as their opponent or even better! I needed to give myself time to deal with my emotions but not now. I wrapped up the conversation with her on a good note, wishing her success in her new endeavors.

"I don't understand the significance of you telling them I was Muslim," I told her. She told me something about "knowing how they are," which I guess insinuated that she was trying to protect me. But I wondered if this was the case or if it was her *reputation* that she wanted to protect. I mean, who wants to be known as the person who put in a good word for a Muslim? But I gave her the benefit of the doubt. Who knows if this was really the case? She encouraged me to still apply for the position. Though I was convinced they already made up their mind; I made the decision to do everything in my power to create favorable results. I knew that we can only get what we work for. It mentions in the Quran in the 39th verse of Surah 53: "Man can only get what he works for." So I intended to give it my all and let them get to know the "real me" without the pre-conceived notions and labels.

I wasn't mad at my colleague; I accepted what happened and moved on. It was an eye-opener and a major learning experience. At the end of the day, if I was meant to get the job, I'll get it, regardless of what she or anyone else said. It's in Allah's hands and everything that will happen is already written; we just have to make sure we make the right decisions.

I made it my mission to be so sharp that they had no choice but to feel compelled to hire me. I went above and beyond critiquing my resume. Even when I was certain there was no mistakes, I looked over it again and got a fresh pair of eyes to examine it.

The former editor-in-chief was very helpful in aiding me through the revision process. I was grateful for her assistance and I felt indebted for all the things I learned from her over the years. I didn't condemn her for what she said to her boss; only Allah knows her intentions and her heart, not me.

I was appreciative that Allah allowed me to construct a flawless resume and cover letter. I put my heart into writing the ultimate cover letter without any embellishing. After devoting hours upon hours on my resume and cover letter, I came back with fresh eyes, only to look for more ways to make more improvements. I must have thrown away thousands of papers with printed resumes and cover letters. After reviewing, critiquing and editing and reaching a point of absolute satisfaction, I printed the final product on the best resume paper available and put it in a fancy resume folder and enclosed it in a matching envelope particularly meant for resumes.

The result: I didn't get the job and wasn't even called for an interview. But it's o.k. because I prepared myself for it. It turn out that Allah saved me from having that job because he had something better in store for me. He blessed me to take a tutoring position at my former college where I would get paid more than at the newspaper and most importantly, gain valuable teaching experience that would prove very fruitful. So everything worked out in my favor anyway! Also, that would be the last time I would seek a position in the journalism field, turning me in a totally different direction that I fell in love with. So I thank Allah for not decreeing for them to hire me. It just confirmed how valuable it is to believe in the All Knower and not lose faith when things seem like they're not going our way.

I sat in one of the seats nearer to the podium and listened attentively to the Shayk give the seminar. I was taking an Islamic class on the branches of eman and I was super-enthused; this is what I lived for, to be able to devote my attention to the studies of the Qur'an and Sunnah without something else stealing my attention. I was finished with school and I left my job. Now attending Islamic classes would take first precedence and I had the flexibility of including invaluable things in my schedule like spending more time reading the transcendent verses of the Qur'an and pondering on them. There was nothing like this feeling!

"Oh! There she is!" an excited voice cried out. I turned around from the vending machine and saw two sisters smiling at me.

I was surprised. "You were looking for me?" I asked, almost in a state of confusion. I had never met the two sisters prior to their approaching me.

"There's a brother interested in you!" one of the sisters responded.

"What?!"

Apparently a brother from the class took interest in me but I had no idea. He told his friend to ask his mother to ask about me. I could hardly believe it. I came to learn, not expecting to link up with a brother. I had no idea who the brother was or what he was about but I wasn't worried. Allah knew if he was suitable for me or not; all I had to do was plug into him and ask him for guidance.

Chapter 5

"Verily, he who fears Allah with obedience to Him and is patient, then surely, Allah makes not the reward of good doers to be lost." (12:90)

Everyone was seated in the Masjid, waiting for me to make my grand entrance.

My mom turned to me before walking in and asked with a bright smile: "Are you ready?" I exhaled.

As I walked in, I heard a synchronized hum of: AWWW! From their reaction, I'm guessing they were blown away by my wedding dress. I briskly walked to the front of the Masjid to meet my father, the Imam and my husband to be who had been waiting for quite some time for me to arrive.

My dress was white with elaborate pink trimmings sprinkled throughout. To top it off, I wore a sparkling crown that my mother had brought for me. Yes, after 25 years, this little princess was about to join a union and embark upon womanhood.

We courted for about a year; we quizzed each other about our convictions, ideas and standards and had a general sketch of our plans together as we planned for a family. We didn't agree on everything but we were o.k. with that; at least we were on the same page and we were willing to work with one another and compromise.

My sister tightly embraced me. "I'm gonna miss you!"

I gave my last hugs to my family and friends and we made our exit out of the Masjid. But after our driver raced us to the airport and we waited on line and got clearance through security, we were in for a major surprise. The time printed on our e-tickets was wrong! While we thought we made good timing, the departure time was actually 30 minutes before we were ready to board. What were we going to do? We had two, non-refundable, one—way tickets to Egypt.

But something unbelievable happened. By the grace and mercy of Allah, we made it on that plane! They had made a couple of announcements for the two missing people to board the flight and although we didn't surface, something stopped the pilot from flying. It was so clear that it was none but the High Almighty delaying the flight for us. We were meant to be on that flight and Allah above had something in store for us!

Coming to Egypt for the first time was an incredible experience! Once arriving in Cairo, nicknamed "Little New York" for its' bright lights, highly polluted areas and large tourist attraction, we didn't feel far from home. Upon arriving at our hotel we immediately prayed to our Lord and showed gratitude for the enormous blessings. How could we sufficiently thank Him for all the blessings He's poured on us from the beginning; guiding us to go to Egypt, making everything smooth for us, saving us from missing our plane. Just the blessing of allowing us to meet the way He did, allowing the families to gel so perfectly and peacefully work together for the benefit of us two, and allow us to actually get married and have a flawless wedding day, was enough to keep us in sujud for a lifetime and that was just the beginning. What more could we ask for? I was extra appreciative that my Lord blessed me with such a great husband who was perfect for me. He was compassionate, humble and serious about his deen. His bottom line was Qur'an and Sunnah and I loved that; and what's more, he gave me the encouragement and assistance when I needed it. After all that time, not knowing when or if I would find that special one, Allah was saving him for me at this appointed time. After 25 years of singlehood, the time had finally arrived. After feeling like I was getting close and then nothing, being disappointed a couple of times, and then witnessing that Allah was not teasing me, but He was saving a huge blessing for me at the time I was ready for it! Not only that but he removed something from me and granted me a replacement 10 times better than what I was willing to accept. Even though at the time, I didn't see it as settling, after growing and developing, it was clear that Allah was promoting me and supporting me with a mate better matched for me. Allah is so Akbar! I went from attending other people's wedding, wondering when my day was going to come to finally attending my own wedding and not wishing that it would have arrived a day sooner.

"The best gift you can give your husband is your virginity," my sister told me. "Imagine how special he'll feel knowing that he's the only one you've been intimate with." These words stayed with me and helped strengthen me during the times that I wasn't sure if I would actually meet my special life partner. I was so grateful that Allah protected me from the worries of sexual transmitted diseases and pre-mature pregnancies and that I was able to focus on myself instead of being distracted having boyfriends and indulging in "fairy tale love." Abstinence wasn't easy but it gave the marriage something more to be appreciated and anticipated. To me, preserving your chastity for your life-long partner, someone who was willing to commit to you and respect you, had way more perks that the "freedom" of going from one person to the next until you get tired and feel the need to settle down.

I accompanied my husband to from time to time when he went to the Masjid for Salah. The feeling of praying Fajr in the Masjid was like no other; I felt invigorated and energized and ready and to start my entire day.

There was nothing like being able to spend as long as I wanted in Salah without feeling the pressure of getting up and getting back to work, school, get a paper done or take care of some matter that demanded my time. I felt myself developing an intimacy with Allah as I recited the glorious words of the Qur'an slowly in prayer, taking care to pronounce slowly while contemplating on the meanings. How could I adequately thank Allah for all the blessings that he showered on me: for blessing me to get married and travel to Egypt, two things I only dreamed about! Going to a Muslim country alone was something that I've wanted to do for so long, and now being about to do so with my new husband was a two-fold blessing. After exerting the patience, the discipline, focus, forbidding myself from blindly following others and choosing to remain faithful, look at the results; when I least suspected it, the opportunity to travel and the mate, with whom I would be traveling with was waiting for me.

After making Salah, I remained on the prayer rug recounting all the blessings visible to me, which I realized was only a fraction of all the blessings my Lord has poured over me. I thanked Allah repeatedly. Being able to realize my dream was one part, but what about my good health, being sheltered and protected, nourished with food and given great parents who did the best they could with what they had. But out of all of that, I think the things most deserving of my faith was growing up with a faith that has been known to move mountains.

After staying in Cairo for about a week, we took a train to Alexandria where we would stay on campus. Allah blessed Muhammad to find out an excellent school where he would get certified to teach English as a second language. Soon the honey moon period was over and my husband was feeling the pressure; after he finished the program he had to secure a job, a place for us and manage our affairs in a foreign country. Islam mandates men as the maintainers and protectors of women; so while I have the choice of working or not, the strain of protecting and leading the family rests on his shoulders. He will be questioned about what he did or didn't do to keep the family afloat and God forbid if anyone drowned while under his watch. What pressure it was to be the leader of the family?! Especially for him, being that we were so far away from family and loved ones who would not want to hear about anything happened.

Muhammad was finishing up the program and the time was ticking for us to find a new place. After talking to someone from the States who used to live in Egypt, we understood that you could be taken for a ride if you're not careful. We were in a difficult position because we didn't know anyone in Egypt personally; we had a few contacts, "friends of a friend" but no one who we ever met in person. One of our contacts from the States told us to let him know what area we were looking to rent and he'll contact the people he knows and try to assist us to the best of our ability. But even this was a standstill because we couldn't even give him an area that we were interested in. Where did we want to live? Cairo? Alexandria? We had no clue. It will all depend on where my husband found work and that was a challenge in itself? We learned that his "limitations" in his educational background and lack of teaching experience was counted against him. Teaching English was quite competitive over here and he needed to stand out. He was lagging behind in the race and in a scuttle to get acclimated with the society and get ourselves established, something needed to be done.

I jazzed up Muhammad's resume, helped him compose dynamite cover letters, researched job opportunities and sent out CV. Almost every time you turned around, I was on that laptop. In the process of searching, I found plenty of positions that I was qualified for; I fulfilled the educational requirements and I had the teaching experience but I wasn't sure if I really wanted to work? I was still enjoying being liberated from work, school and other responsibilities that stole my time. Now I was a newlywed and I wanted to enjoy it for a minute. Also, I was hyped about embarking on my studies; this is what I was waiting my entire life for and finally it was here. Did I want to make a commitment to a 9 to 5 that could possibly distract me or convert my experience from a joyful one into a daunting one? Also, would I be able to work and upkeep the house and other new responsibilities that came with being a wife, while optimistically keeping up with my studies, without feeling burdened and drained. I was still adjusting to my new "role" as wife and that seemed to be enough on my plate, did I want to add something else that would require more discipline on my part? On the other hand, maybe this would be a help to me? I definitely knew it would help my husband and help us financially and the blessings that come from that could be never ending. Could this be an opportunity to go outside of myself and reach a higher level? I was unsure. I asked Allah to show me the way.

My husband and I needed to find a place and no job opportunities were coming through yet. Me picking up a job seemed more and more like an option. I continued to send my husband's resume out and pay attention to any signs Allah may be giving me.

Muhammad met someone who knew of an apartment we could rent. Then someone else knew about another place and then another. Allah kept putting people in his path with better deals than the previous ones. The first place we knew about would be more than 1,000 Egyptian Pounds a month, the next one cheaper, and the next one even cheaper and we ended up moving into a place which only cost us only 300 Pounds a month to rent. Allahu Akbar!

Within a week after getting acclimated into our new home, Muhammad met some really helpful brothers who extended themselves to him. Many of them invited us to their homes and I got a chance to meet their wives. It was truly a blessing and comfort to have people welcome us so genuinely.

The next thing was trying to secure a job for my husband. We had some savings but we didn't want to touch it unless we absolutely had to and even so, we couldn't live on that forever. Muhammad continued to search and I continued to send his resume out as well. I could tell he was getting discouraged. "Don't worry, Allah got us," I reassured him. I knew he believed that but we all need a reminder at times. We talked about the possibility of me working and I told him I would make Salatul Istakharah. I forgot about the urgency of us being financially secure, and was not swayed by any outside influence. I prayed to Allah and sat in a quiet place. Allah is Ar-Razzaq, I assured myself and even if I don't go out there and work, I know He'll provide for us. The question was, is this something I really wanted to do right now. Would it aid me in getting closer to my Lord and fulfilling my mission or would it derail me from it? I sat and listened.

"No! I'm not gonna do it," I told my husband. He looked a little disappointed but I had to stick to my guns. If I ask Allah for the answer, I have to go with it; He knows and we know not.

Working outside of the home may have seemed to be the easy way out but I knew what would happen if I chose to work at that time. Allah was giving me a clear sign that working now wasn't best and I wasn't going to pretend that I knew better.

Muhammad was looking sharp! He had on his nice dress shirt and his dress pants, his kufi and he was ready to go. He left the house early in the morning looking for work and came back in the evening with nothing, only to go back to the drawing board and start fresh again. One day he accompanied some brothers from the neighborhood to check out some schools.

"There are schools right in the neighborhood," the brothers told him.

So Muhammad planned a trip to the schools early in a morning. By this time, I started to feel bad for him face rejection, after rejection and become a little less hopeful. I started to see these trips as a useless, waste of time. What were the odds that he was going to find something? But regardless, I only expressed positivity. I hid my pessimism, kissed him before leaving the house and offered some encouraging words. Deep down inside, I knew Allah would take care of it; I wasn't sure when but I was confident it'll eventually happen.

It never occurred to me that it would happen so soon! My husband came home smiling from ear to ear. "What happened?"

One of the Middle Schools he visited hired him on the spot. It turns out they were in need of an English teacher and since Muhammad was American, they were overzealous about having him join their team. Allahu Akbar! It was all worth it! The hard work, diligence and me holding out. It was nothing like letting him have the satisfaction of going out there and do his duty as a man; finding the risq that was written for him so that he could support his family. I could have gone out there and work until he found something but I knew what that would have meant; not having me bring in any income pushed him to do what he had to do to make it happen. There was nothing like witnessing that wonder up front in center! It reassured us that it had nothing to do with luck at all; this was no coincidence, Allah wrote that Muhammad would be teaching there and nobody or nothing could stop it. His educational background didn't matter and his lack of teaching experience didn't count. The criteria for selecting teachers and the usual screening process did not prevent him from getting something that Allah had for him. I was ecstatic and so grateful to Allah for allowing us to witness such a miracle. How could he have known that this school was looking for a teacher, which happened to be in walking distance from our new home, which we would have never gotten, if it hadn't been for Allah. Which of the favors of your Lord do you deny?!

I walked out of the house covering my face for the first time. I had wanted to try wearing the niqab in the States but was never courageous enough to try it. I knew I had better be prepared for the stares, comments and the hostility and I didn't want to bring on extra adversaries if I could help it. Now being in an Islamic environment, eliminated all of my worries. I could try wearing the niqab in peace and determine if I wanted to take on this practice without being swayed by feelings of discomfort. It felt good, being able to wear it and not get treated any different from those around me. I walked through the streets happily greeting everyone with "Assalamualaikum" and getting a cheery response back. I covered my entire face except my eyes and it was quite an adjustment. I had to keep telling myself that I could breathe fine, which was really the truth; it was just a mental thing, since my nose was covered and I wasn't used to it. Anytime we embark on a new endeavor we can expect it to be some discomfort but I didn't truly comprehend this at the time so after wearing it a couple of times I took it off. I wasn't really sure if I wanted to wear it anyway and any inclination that this would make life harder for me was not motivation to make an upgrade, even if it was something that would enable me to earn more rewards with my Lord and possibly a higher status if coupled with sincere intentions.

Once I took the niqab off, I started getting more attention from those who I became immune from while covering my face. In one instance, while in a computer lab at my husband's school, I found myself almost the "center" of attention whereby, it seemed as if every five minutes an excuse was made to strike up a conversation with me, so that they have a reason to stare at my face. Either they were captivated by my beauty or the capability of being able to see my face astonished them. Then I understood the fitna that came along with the beauty of a woman. My head was covered and I was able to get such a response, imagine what the case would have been if more were revealed. This is why a woman can go out in the streets dressed a certain way and stop traffic, whereas a man can be half-naked and not even get a partial response that a woman may get. While a woman has a choice to wear what they please, no one can deny that it is called adornments for a reason.

I know that man is weak, which is why it makes sense for me to use a means of prevention to protect myself. Though men should be able to control themselves, even if presented with a woman, the reality is there are sick men out there who either cannot or choose not to control themselves, which would be equivalent to putting a juicy piece of steak in front of a starving dog and expecting them not to bite. If you don't realize that the dog is hungry, you may use caution or at least wisdom.

This is where the Qur'an comes in. The Qur'an is the last revelation sent from God to mankind; it is a means of communication whereby the Creator is warning us and advising us. Any commandments or prohibitions are given to us are only for our own good; if we choose to disobey, we will have to bear the consequences. Many of the prohibitions in the Qur'an are the similar to those instructed in the Bible, as it has the same author, God.

Growing up in Islam and covering my hair was a piece of cake and became second nature. I knew that if I didn't do it then I'd be sinning and I'd have to answer to Allah for it. On the other hand, if I *did* do it, then every time I wore it, I would receive a reward from Allah. I was tested and if I passed the test and remained steadfast, Insha Allah, I could look forward to entering Paradise where I could do whatever I wanted and would *not* have to cover my hair or have any restrictions on what I wore. Wearing a hijab is obligatory at minimum but anyone who wanted to take it a step further and wear a niqab as well, then they would earn extra blessings and rewards from Allah.

Not long after the incident in the computer lab, I decided to wear the niqab full-time, that is, wear it whenever I was in public. It was hard to adjust at first but I reminded myself why I was doing it and before you knew it, it became second nature like wearing the hijab was. Covering was only a means of protection in the outside world full of predators and sick men but when I got home, I took off my hijab and niqab and was able to remove my clothes and beautify myself for my husband, after all, he is the one who I feel comfortable showing my adornments to, not some strange men.

They were able to host me without taking any attention away from their husbands, always "checking in" on them and asking them if everything o.k. There was a constant revolving motion of dishes on the table; they set an elaborate display of fancy dishes on the table, fixed the plate for them, removed the dishes when they finished eating and replaced them with seconds and thirds on demand. They came back with tea, smoothies, sweets, you name it! I was in awe. I never saw anything like this! Where I come from, the woman may make their husband's plate and they may even get them something from the fridge upon request, but she's not making a hobby out of sitting there before you smiling, asking if there was anything they can do to make your meal—taking experience even more enjoyable; she cooked it, so you better be satisfied, otherwise, you have feet, and you can use them to get whatever else you want! Watching how the Egyptian women did things made me appreciate their loving and generous spirit, but I must admit that I felt like a lower breed in their presence.

Look at where they are compared to me. I resented doing any chores or any other "duty" if I thought it took too much of my time and I didn't really like serving my husband. A part of me felt like, at that moment, I was more like his servant rather than his partner. Why should I go out my way to constantly bring him stuff from the kitchen, when he can just do it himself? I didn't get it! Why did these women do all that? Is this how a real Muslim woman should be? Was my "lack" of service to my husband a reflection of my "lack" of faith? I didn't know. I tended to get an attitude, whereas my Egyptian sisters had the pleasant disposition where they made it their duty to please their husband, family and guests.

The interesting thing is, when it came down to someone else, my mother, sister or friend, I had no problem fulfilling requests for them with a smile but when it came to my husband, something was preventing me from fully embracing him. I didn't like feeling like a maid and I didn't like feeling like I had to plan my day around him and his wishes. I didn't like the feeling of him interrupting me from my agenda, no matter how beneficial the task may be, even though I benefitted from it. It wasn't long until I realized what was happening to me. I was re-playing the damaging, subconscious thought: "I don't want to re-live the life of my mother."

My husband liked things to be in order and understandably so but sometimes I would let the work pile up, making it harder on him and me. It was hard for him to function in dysfunction but to me, it was just a few things out of place so I didn't see it as a big deal. However, by procrastinating, I made the job bigger than it was, rather than just cleaning a little bit at a time. Unknowingly, I rolled my eyes when he reminded me how important it was to be organized and keep things in an order. Why doesn't he get off my back, I thought to myself, I'm going to get to it, not understanding the magnificence of my actions and what I was doing. All I knew was I was giving my all trying to discipline my nafs and be obedient to my husband for the pleasure of Allah but it was hard!

Even when there weren't a lot of chores to do, I still resented it. Why do I have to this maid work? I never said it to my husband but that's what I felt. It was boring and monotonous! I didn't like the idea of me "having" to do anything. I wanted to do what I pleased, when I pleased. Wait a minute! I knew I had to be fair. What if Muhammad had the same attitude as me when it came to working? What if he had an attitude about working and "having" to maintain me? What if he just refused to go to work, except only when he felt like it? I didn't have to worry about going out there and providing for the family. I had the option of staying home or working and if I did work, I didn't have to worry about paying the bills unless I wanted to help out and I would be rewarded for doing so. Sometimes we all have to do things that we may not be particularly happy about. Our nafs wants to have paradise on earth but we have to struggle until Insha'Allah, Allah permits us to paradise and then for eternity, there's no worrying about disciplining our nafs, just indulging in pleasures! But until then, we have to be careful because trying to indulge now without adhering to the boundaries comes with consequences; Allah knows what's best for us and we weren't designed for that reason. Still, even knowing this didn't make struggling against my nafs any more enjoyable.

I didn't like cleaning, I wasn't a fan of cooking and I hated washing clothes mainly because it required so much effort and energy; we didn't have an automatic wash machine which made washing a mult-step process: pre-washing to get stains out, putting it in the wash machine, lifting the wash machine and letting it down to release the clothes, rinsing it, ringing it dry and then hanging them out on the line to dry. It was exhausting! And the whole way through I had to motivate myself to keep going. When it was over I needed to recuperate only to motivate myself to complete another task. Why am I here? Like many people, I like being married but I don't like the work that comes with it. But it's going to take work if I truly want a long lasting, successful marriage. I could either go back to the single life where I could do as I pleased or fully embark on this journey of cooperation and respect, where I discipline my nafs and give just as I expected to take. The same he choice was mine.

The problem would remain there and my condition would worsen. I already had an attitude with my husband and I had some deep issues to deal with in terms of my perception and expectation of men, and what I learned about marriage from my mother and father at an early age. With something simple just as house chores, took twice the work because of the mental barriers that I had to wrestle with, and the resistance to be "happy Suzzy maker." I didn't like myself too much with this disposition. I wanted to radiate warmth in the home, not wretchedness but in a sense I didn't know how. "You get more bees with honey," I remember my mother always saying. I wished I could be sweeter but until the bitterness at the core was deal with, I couldn't be so sweet to my husband all the time. I had limits and still hadn't knocked down all the walls.

Why should I be the one to shut my mouth, when I know I'm right? I thought to myself. My husband and I were having another argument. While he was calm and talked with a mild tone, I raised my voice and cut him off repeatedly. He looked perturbed; I could tell he was really trying to compose himself. He finally ended the "conversation" and let me get the last word. I felt bad. Why wasn't I able to do that, just smile and let him get the last word? Somewhere in my subconscious mind I was telling myself that if I did that, I would be allowing him to overpower me and thus be submissive, something I vowed never to do. But was that really the case, I asked myself. All I knew was, my actions weren't getting me anywhere.

Most times, at the end of the day when it was time to go to bed, I felt him being angry with me without even saying anything. He would sleep with his back turned away from me. That hurt! But was it enough to spark me to make a change? I was still troubled by my convictions on what to expect from your husband after being committed and vulnerable. I wanted to trash them but how could I without replacing it with something better and something better that I truly believed in? I read about the companions of the Prophet Muhammad (peace and blessings be upon him) and how respectful the wives were with their husbands but they were practically perfect and look at me. Could I ever be on the same level as them and have the same poise as them? My idealistic view of marriage has not only been altered but shattered. How can I ever get that back? And relationship between me and my husband has been battered, was there any hope for things turning around?

I was happy Muhammad spent most of the day out of the house and when he came home, neither of us were excited to see each other. We barely talked to each other, it seems without arguing. I thought he was being too critical of me; he always had these suggestions of what I should do. It seemed as if he was disappointed that I hadn't yet picked up on my "wife intuition" and evolved beyond being self-centered. It's true. While at the time I didn't see it, he was absolutely right. When he got home, my habits would barely change. If I was on the computer, I stayed there for long amounts of time without asking when he would be ready for dinner or even taking myself out of my world to think about him for a couple of minutes. Since I was so focused on maintaining my "power," I didn't realize that it had nothing to do with being subservient; it was simply about being kind and thinking about someone else, someone who happened to be one of the most valuable people in my life. But my mind revisited the Egyptian women who so happily served those around her without even thinking about it. This is what he wants to change me into, I thought to myself, and the walls shot up. Should I constantly surround my day around him and doing things that he wants done? That's the most boring thing in the world! I don't want to do that. Is this a level that I should aspire to reach as a Muslim woman, where I am content by simply staying in the home all day and surrounding my life around my husband? I mean, I stay in the home by default, because I choose not to work at this time, but am I really happy playing this role? If not, what was the root issue that caused such displeasure? And how do I find the cure? Something has to happen because neither of us were happy.

"What's wrong?" I asked my husband.

"I don't wanna go back to that place!" he said in a melancholy tone as if he was being dragged to his death. He sat at the kitchen table with a dismal look on his face. I felt so bad for him. I knew there were issues at his job but I didn't realize the effects this was having on him. It didn't seem like a good fit at all and he was seriously contemplating leaving but the responsibility of taking care of the family must always be considered for the breadwinner.

At that moment I realized how much stress he was feeling from his job. For the first time I would care to inquire about his feelings and attempt to soothe him, as opposed to responding to his ill-fit mood by being defensive, as a result of feeling guilty for causing an alter in his mood. As a result, I had responded to his despondency with dissent rather than love. This incident was a turning point; it caused me to be more cognizant of my attitude towards him and motivated me to be less defensive and more kind to him. He really deserved it. He was a fantastic husband; he always showed concern for me and my feelings even though I didn't always deserve it and he was there for me in every way that he could. It was time for me to exert some real effort in treating him better. He was worth it. After all, this is the only person I deemed worthy enough to make a commitment to, my first and hopefully my last, if I could just get it together.

Usually after jumping rope, I was more revved up to take care of chores and do the cooking. I challenged myself to do fulfill a time limit before being satisfied and putting down the rope. Starting these tasks after attaining a sense of accomplishment and joy was wondrous! It was like giving myself a pep talk. I'm doing this to please Allah, I reminded myself. I know you rather be doing ibada but this is ibada, and I can't think that by sitting around praying and reading the Qur'an to the neglect my 'amana is pleasing to Allah. It's not the most enjoyable things to do but my account is being filled with blessings and my husband and I will both benefit. Alhumdulillah.

Out of all the people I ever met, no one made an impression on me like Um Osama, that is the mother of Osama, not the person who gained famed one September 11 but the mother of a common Egyptian brother who happened to be friends with my husband. There was no relationship to my husband's friend, Osama and the Saudi Osama Bin Laden. In fact, Osama didn't even know him, in case you're wondering. Muhammad met him soon after we moved to our new place; he lived with his parents right across from us.

Um Osama welcomed us our first night there sending us some delicious Egyptian dishes. Not yet having our stove working yet, we really appreciated the hospitality. It was no accident that I met Um Osama. I got to know her personally as she hosted me over her house, taught me how to cook some Egyptian dishes and shared jewels with me in the form of life experience and wisdom with me upon request.

I never met anyone like Um Osama. She was the epitome of sincerity, generosity, humility and strength. She didn't have not one negative bone in her body and she always said things in the best way, devoid of any criticism, judgment or abhorrence. She stood out from all the Egyptian women I met because she had a strong identity outside of a mother and wife; she was able to be who she was without any quarrels and everyone loved being able around her; we appreciated her genuineness; she wasn't fulfilling some duty because it was prescribed on her by her culture, having an amazing Aqlaq became a part of her. She worked outside of the home and that did not prevent her from being just as hospitable and devoting as the rest of the Egyptian women; in fact, she topped all of them, being the most cheerful, hardworking and patient than all of them put together. She lived to serve Allah in the best way she could, exemplifying the highest standard of character I've ever seen. Um Osama was my shero; she was the living role model that I needed to examine up in person.

I didn't feel like a low-breed being in her presence at all probably because I didn't have a distant relationship with her. Upon just coming to Egypt and learning about the way the women did it was intimidating but the more evolved I became and the more I reflected and gradually improved my service to my husband, the less intimidated I was. Knowing Um Osama up close and personal put me more at ease and helped me not to be envious of Egyptian women for having the "training" that I never got. I still thought I was at a great disadvantage because of my background, my parent's divorce and the consequent not so positive advice given from my mother, but I was beginning to chip at the wall which had been built for so long and I was making progress day by day. I wasn't able to go back in time and change the past but I was able to put the work in now for a brighter future. I had some serious constructive therapy to do on myself but it was worth it; I was motivated to demolish the destructive habits and build a sturdy foundation, whereby I would attain peace within myself, in my marriage and do my part to raise healthy, spiritually-fortified children who hopefully won't have to go through the same thing that I did. Having Um Osama as a mother figure, someone who imparted astuteness on me and showed me so much by example was a major gift from Allah that I will always treasure!

Um Osama will go down in history as being my only friend over the age of 50. This huge age gap did not make me embarrassed or compel me to downgrade her friendship at all. It didn't make any difference to me, as a matter of fact it was a plus having someone in my circle with such great experience and insight. I felt honored to be in her presence and to witness how she was able to get it all done so gracefully: husband, children, grandchildren, career, keeping ties with her family members, being involved in the community, the true definition of balance! I admired her for that and for the work she did. In addition, she worked in such a healthy and gratifying profession; she had the best job in the world! She was able to affect change, motivate, inspire, and make a positive impact on individuals every single day that she went to work. What did she do for a living? She was a Qur'an teacher.

I happily stepped out of our apartment on my way to the Mahad. A friend from Muhammad's job told him about the four-year Islamic studies program there and he enrolled both of us. I went from home and he went from his job on Fridays. We attended on Fridays and Saturdays and it was the most fantastic thing in the world, outside of reciting the Qur'an. It reminded me of the days I took classes with Al Maghrib, a course for per double weekend. Now I could take a course for an entire semester and study more in depth. That's what I'm talking about! I was ready to sink my teeth in. This is what I wanted and now I had it. Allah is so Akbar!

Chapter 6

It may be that you dislike something while it is good for you; and it may be that you love something while it is bad for you. And Allah knows while you do not know. (Qur'an 2:216)

"You're gonna have baby there or in the States," my brother asked me over the phone.

I didn't have a clue. "Allah knows best," I told him.

We had already been in Egypt a little bit over a year and just the idea of going back to the U.S. and seeing my family made me jubilant, and the thought of them being there for the birth of the baby was delightful! Feeling the way that I was, I knew that if I left Egypt, most likely I wouldn't be back. My excitement about living there was steadily declining and I was started to wonder if I really wanted to spend the rest of my life over here. My husband tried to get me to recall the good things I liked about the country. I wasn't disregarding my blessings. There were a lot of good things about the place but I wasn't sure if it was emotions from the pregnancy or if I was at the point of re-considering my needs and what's important to me. No doubt about it, my husband didn't want to go anywhere but even he was having feelings of homesickness; it came up when we were discussing my condition. I wasn't sure if I was homesick but I was starting to feel sick and tired, I don't know if it was of my environment or just life in general. I felt trapped in a boring routine when I looked around there wasn't much to get me excited. I woke up, cooked, cleaned, and went to bed, only to wake up the next day and do it all again. Not all days were the same, some days I managed to get some studying in and from time to time and my husband went out, visiting friends or something of that nature; those days were the highlighted for me. I felt like a wave, being pushed by the current of wind called life, just merely existing.

"You gotta get out," Muhammad told me.

"Where" I asked.

He recommended I go over take a trip to the sea, near his old school. It was a fabulous idea. It was a tourist site; they had benches where you could see the sea below and it was a beautiful, captivating view. I took the public mashoor and made spontaneous trips over there. It was a great feeling just walking the board walk and letting myself go in the breeze. Other times I would visit his old school to watch educational videos on Islamic topics and use the internet. I refrained from telling my family about my struggle; they were already concerned about the new baby being on the way, the last thing I wanted to do was give them more to worry about. I would be fine eventually; I just had to ride the waves during this brief time of turmoil. I wasn't sure exactly what was going on with me but all I knew was I was pregnant for the first time and the hormones were kicking my butt.

We were getting pressure from my family to come to the U.S.; the thought of having a baby in a foreign land did not sit well with most of them, especially my mother. Every time I turned around she was e-mailing me or sending me messages, trying to convince me how it'll be more beneficial to deliver in the U.S.

"How many months are you?" my stepmother asked me on the other end of the line.

"I just gave birth."

"What!!!"

All I remember is the nurse telling me to breathe a couple of times and the next thing you know, I woke up with my husband on the edge of my bed and Um Osama and Um Muhammad, the mother of Muhammad's friend who happened to live a couple of blocks from me and who I grew a great repo re with, sitting a couple of feet away from me. Giving birth for the first time was so easy and smooth. Allah is so Akbar!

I had this little life that was charged under my care. I was now a mother! She would look to me to feed her, nourish her, love her and guide her. Would I raise her to be an Egyptian who loved to serve her husband and devote herself in her home solely, raising the kids and taking care of the home or would I teach her to be independent, ambitious and career-driven? Should I direct her to be content staying in the home, instead of encouraging her to go out there and empower herself with an education like mom did with us? And if I did, what would that do for her if she is raised here in Egypt? If she is influenced by the culture to do otherwise, would she find herself resenting the culture or resenting me and what I taught her? I was so confused. I didn't really know what I wanted for my daughter because I didn't really know what I wanted for myself. I found myself being frustrated for being a square and not being able to fit into a circle. But what if I didn't want to be a circle but felt like I had to? One thing for sure, I didn't want my daughter to have to go through this! I wanted her to be at peace and feel comfortable being herself regardless.

Since there were no complications during the pregnancy and I was perfectly fine I could go home the same day. A part of me wished I could stay in the hospital a couple of days; the thought of going back home and having to get back to "work" wasn't appealing. I just wished I could enjoy spending quality time with my new baby without being tied down to a billion and one responsibilities. I was already having a hard time keeping up with everything before I gave birth, now factor in feeding a baby every two hours, changing her diapers, cleaning her, giving her comfort when she cries and dropping everything to respond to her urgent needs right away. When would I have time to bond with my baby and enjoy motherhood.

Well, Alhumdulillah, my dua was answered without me even having to make it. The day I came home from the hospital, Um Osama gave us a large container of chicken soup; that lasted a couple of days. Um Muhammad, the other sister who was there for me during my birth took it upon herself to bring over some more food which lasted nearly half a week. It was such a blessing to have good sisters in my path who sincerely cared for me and did everything they could to help me.

Not only that, but something spectacular happened. When I came home from the hospital my husband alleviated me from doing all the cooking and cleaning and happily granted me the privilege of enjoying my new baby. For four and a half weeks I was able to bond with little Aisha, take my time feeding her without being bombarded with a list of things to take care of, go to sleep feeling rested, waking up for Fajr and then go back for more sleep without it being interrupted by the dreaded alarm clock. Allah is so Akbar!

Muhammad came to the bedroom with my meals, drinks and anything else I needed. He frequently asked me if I desired anything and didn't delay in carrying out the requests. His stupendous service melted my heart! Though I had given him an attitude through at least half the marriage and I barely served him with half of the care he did, this didn't prevent him from outdoing himself in trying to please me. When he entered the room, his face lit up as if he really did adored serving me. He prepared my favorite dishes, asked me if I wanted seconds and cared enough to switch things up to give me variety, knowing that after a while I get tired of having the same thing over and over again; if I have to do it, I'll endure it without complaining about it but it wasn't my favorite thing. He put me to shame. I felt incredibly guilty. I don't deserve all this, I thought to myself. Yet, even after what I put him through, he maintained a high standard of aqlaq. I thought back to the Egyptian women who went above and beyond for their husbands. I had qualms about them having this type of high performance when serving their husbands but why didn't I have a problem with my husband doing so. It's all about interpretation; if a woman does it, I saw them as being oppressed, but the last word I would use to describe Muhammad would be oppressed. He chose to go above and beyond to treat his wife kindly, just like the Egyptian women did. No one was forcing them to do that; it was encouraged in their culture but that's understandable because traditionally they don't work outside the home. The way they see it, the man goes out and provides and the women takes care of the home, so many of them pride themselves in being their best at their job. Though I don't think there's nothing wrong with that, somehow in my mind I had been equating women being dutiful to being subservient. I re-visited what I saw take place between my parents and then understood why. Now that I recognized what happened to me psychologically, and my husband showed me there's no reason for me to resent serving him and in fact he was willing to serve me with no problem, I was faced with the daunting task of finding the courage to release myself from bondage. I didn't want to have an attitude with my husband and I didn't want to view cooking, cleaning and being nice to my husband as servitude but I had been convinced this for so long. The thought of being too "accessible" didn't sit well with me, until now. I knew my husband wasn't the type to take advantage of anyone at all, especially not his wife. But regardless how much he showed me I didn't have to worry about this, my deep-ridden subconscious thoughts made me feel a need to protect myself. If my husband's kind treatment and exceptional service to me wasn't convincing enough that it was time to drop those negative expectations and reform my thoughts, what else was there?

I was motivated to show as much care in serving my husband as he did serving me after giving birth. Once I got back on my feet, I envisioned myself taking care of everything and not regardless of how I stressed I was, not taking it out on him or trying my best not to let it show. I shouldn't put a damper on his mood because of whatever I was struggling with. But something happened, I had a high expectation but I didn't consider where I was at and how long it would take me to get there. It's like going from C to Z in a week. No matter how much effort you exert, it's not going to happen! I needed to set milestones and draft out a plan, including how I can deal with getting back up when I fell, because it's not a matter "if" you're going to fall but when. So, after four and a half weeks of not doing any cleaning and cooking I abruptly went back to managing the household and taking care of a new born all at once. That can be pretty overwhelming for anyone, especially someone in my shoes who had already been struggling with time management and not letting my feelings reflect my service to my husband. As a result, it wasn't long before I got overwhelmed and I was condemning myself for not being able to be the "perfect" Egyptian wife. Who made it obligatory for me to "fulfill" this standard? Not my husband for sure. He encouraged me to strive to be the best overall as a Muslim but he appreciated me for who I was and why wouldn't he, after all, he knew who I was before he decided to marry me. However, I was still under the impression that the "Egyptian's way" of overdoing it was the ideal way a Muslimah wife should be. This meant I was lacking in some type of way and fell behind and according to my knowledge, my background and upbringing prevented me from ever catching up. This was frustrating, always feeling like I had a deficiency and regardless of how much effort I put in it, not feeling content with my level; I had no idea that I was the cause for my own anguish; since I was so busy condemning my past and using the Egyptian woman as a standard I couldn't appreciate where I was or see the beauty of what I went through.

But I was grateful for the progress I was able to make in having a better attitude with my spouse, in being more timely in taking care of the chores and in having a healthier, more positive perspective in general. Yes, it was tough getting it all done but Alhumdulillah, Allah alleviated much difficulty from me when it came time to washing clothes. Allah upgraded us from the manual washer to a washer and spinner; this meant I no longer had the daunting task of empting out the contents after every wash and it eliminated rinsing the clothes and ringing each piece of clothes individually. That was a great relief. Also, Allah really blessed us to do much better financially. We upgraded from eating meat only on the holidays to eating it once a week and sometimes even more frequently. And in no time we replaced boiling water with drinking filtered water from an expensive, irrigation filter system. We had money to go out and do things and we saved. Allah had really blessed us.

I painfully exerted myself in completing all the task of the day and entreated myself to keep work harder until I saw results. I was determined to do things better. I wanted to get to the point where I could check off the tasks at the end of the day instead of them constantly rolling over to the next day and slowing progress. I felt I didn't have the privilege of making time for myself and doing things that I enjoyed like writing, not until I fulfilled all my obligations without any deficiency and or until all the things are checked off completely. I wanted to fly but it seemed like I could never make leeway. As soon as I got into it, something else would come up and interrupt the flow of things. I breast fed the baby every two hours so after nursing her for 45 minutes that only left me 1 hour and 15 minutes to get something done before going back to another feed, not to mention changing, and other things that would always come up. I spent countless amount of times trying to calculate what would be more time efficient. Should I start cooking a meal or sweep the floor? Should I throw a load of clothes in the wash machine or wash the dishes? I wanted to get it all done but sometimes had no idea where to start. There were always things that needed to get done; I felt like I could never get a break. I could tell when Muhammad was annoyed; I knew he did not like when the house wasn't in order; it impeded on his ability to function as it did for me as well. But he was patient and he helped out as much as he could, even with the escalating hours spent at work. I felt bad when he had to ask me to do something but did not get to it due to my poor time management and inability to prioritize. Many times I would just slow down and feel tempted to give.

Everything needs to get done but regardless what I do, at the end of the day some things won't get done, leaving me to go to bed with a weight and wake up with that same burden on my neck. Sometimes I delayed going to bed at a decent hour, seeking to at least get everything taken care of, but of course that would affect me getting a good night's rest and determine how early I was able to wake up. Even if I did come close to completing all the tasks, waking up late would put me behind again and I was back to square one. I reminded myself of women who were able to hold down the household, take care of the kids, plus more. Why wasn't I able to do that? I must be doing something wrong! But I had no idea what it was.

Every morning, I tried it again. I woke up early and started off with high motivation but by mid-day, when I saw things not going much different from the previous days I slowed down; not only did I begin to lose hope but I became exhausted. I had anemia which meant my blood doesn't carry enough oxygen to all the parts of my body, leaving my organs and tissues not working as well as they should. This meant it took me twice as much effort exerting myself than the average person, which left me getting tired quicker and in need of more time to recuperate and muster up the energy to get out there and try again. Shortly after giving birth I wasn't regular taking my pre-natal vitamins and my iron pills. I wasn't convinced that the low-cost pills offered in the drug store were effective so in time I stopped taking them all together. Not taking any measures to replace them, I would pay for it later on.

My husband was now working in Tonta and it took him four hours to travel everyday. From the time he left the house in the morning until he came home at midnight, I was busy at work, looking forward to finishing up what I had to do so I could do a little bit of what I wanted to do. I had the entire day without having to stop my work to tend to my husband and still when he was getting home, often times I still couldn't check off all the items of the day. I was exhausted and not happy knowing that my husband had arrived and I hadn't even had sufficient time to unwind and do nearly as much as I wanted to. Needless to say, I wasn't that happy when my husband got home and I wasn't really in the mood to talk half the time but I pushed myself to have the best treatment that I could. When he asked me about my day, I refrained from complaining and asked him about his day. After working all day, I just wanted to sit down; I was exhausted! But I knew that he had been working all day too for both of us so I got up to offer his meal and make tea for him afterwards. I wish I had some down time for myself. I felt like I was being torn between my husband, my baby, and the countless chores and duties that kept coming up. I was drained and didn't know how much more I could take it. I felt like all the pep was being drained from me.

School was known to aid me in moving around with a little pep, but we still had not commenced after the long break. I noticed a decrease in my energy and need to push myself to get out of bed in the morning. I needed a major pick me up; some days I was more motivated than others. Depriving myself from including activities I enjoyed, many times I felt dead and asking myself what I had to look forward to. Needless to say, the enjoyment of being a mother had been sucked out of me and I became to dread all these "duties" that demanded my time and attention. I began to just go through the motions, living each day being confident that it wouldn't be any different than the previous ones. Hopefully school would start back up again soon.

By the grace of Allah, I did not allow my anguish to damper Muhammad's spirits. I was pleasant with him and I served him with a smile most of the times. The times I was really tested and was unable to be cheery with him, I was able to deal with him in a cordial way without taking out my frustration out on him. I resisted the temptation to be dry and withdrawn with him and tried my best to treat him as I would want him to treat me. When he came home from work, I had dinner ready for him and was attentive. Our relationship had definitely improved drastically. Instead of arguing, we actually talked and I actually was beginning to enjoy his company like in the beginning. We had "video night" where we sat on the coach watched a talk from someone knowledgeable such as a sheikh or a student of knowledge. Most times we popped some popcorn and made some tea to go along with the glance.

I was accustomed to pedaling backwards for so long that it had become automatic. Now I faced the challenge of operating this device in the manner it was designed. I had to purify my mind of the poisonous thoughts and beliefs that had dictated my actions for so long and replace them with healthy, constructive ones so that I would actually move forward. It doesn't matter what I witnessed taking place in my parents' marriage or what anyone said or did. My husband was not my enemy and there was nothing wrong with serving him; it didn't mean I was going to go "overboard" with it like the Egyptians but I would be courageous enough to knock down the walls and try to be a little more open with him. I didn't mean I was subservient or less than; as a matter of fact it made me a humble servant of Allah and nothing could have elevated me to something greater.

I was motivated to go inward and embark on this wonderful transformation; no one else could do the work for me. There were times when I had to stop myself from falling into the same routine of pedaling backwards. There were times when pedaling the right way seemed strange, times when I slowed down and got discouraged but I kept on pedaling and asked God for assistance all throughout the way.

Chapter 7

"You will never attain true faith until you want for your brother what you want for yourself." (Bukhari, volume)

"I want you and the baby to come with me," my husband insisted.

I hesitated as I was sorting through the stacks of book in the living room.

I invited the sister over my house, who just made hijra with her mother. This would only be my second time having a conversation with her and I only got good vibes from her. She struck me as an innocent, sweet Muslimah who only knew good. She was 19 years old, only 6 years younger than me.

I welcomed her to be herself. I had my hijab off and sat on the floor facing the sister, who sat on my coach. I offered her some fruit and some sweet tea and just talked to her. In the beginning, she shied away from accepting anything but after being at my house for at least an hour, she was comfortable enough to ask for some more tea and she felt comfortable enough to have hers off. That's what I wanted, for her to be herself and not feel like she had to act "proper" in front for me. We talked about marriage, Islam and just life in general. At the end of the conversation, I had confirmed my first impression bout her; she seemed like a sweet sister who was really striving to do what is pleasing to Allah.

"What do you think about polygamy? I asked Jamillah.

"I love polygamy!" she answered, causing me to raise my eyebrows but I didn't think much of it.

I asked her what she thought about marrying my husband. Soon she was lit up and excited about the possibility of her getting married. She had expressed a strong desire to get married and the idea of it happening gave her gratification.

After doing a little questioning about how she was considered to marry my husband, I told her the story. She seemed real tough that I thought about her.

"Are you sure?" she asked me.

"I'm sure," I said confidently.

"I really believe when you help other people, you help yourself," I told her.

I explained to her how this arraignment would also be beneficial to me being that I didn't want to move to Tonta.

"So I would be the one to move to Tonta?" she asked.

"Yes," I said without hesitation.

She expressed no resistance to moving and continued to articulate happiness for having the opportunity to do something she's been wanting to do for a while. I knew how it was.

She left my house smiling.

"Thank you," she said and gave me a hug. "I'm going to tell my mother."

A couple of days passed and I haven't heard from her. The next time spoke with her, she was telling me on the phone that she was confused and asked if she could come over my house and ask me some questions.

"Sure," I said without thinking about it.

"When," she asked anxiously. "Monday?"

I wasn't sure if I'd be free as I was studying for exams and nowadays, I had study sessions to attend, business I had to take care outside of the house and general studying. I was sure I had something planned on Monday but I made arrangements to postpone them and accommodate her.

"The only problem I have with your husband is I don't want to move to Tonta," she told me. I wasn't disappointed or mad. If I didn't want to move to Tonta, I shouldn't expect for her to want to either.

My husband and I happened to be in the living room during that particular time; we were enjoying eachother's company. He was looking at a book and I was reclining on the coach, looking at my notes on and off while we were conversing. It was a Friday and he was off from work.

After I relayed the news to him about Jamillah not wanting to move, you could see the reaction on his face.

"Nobody wants to move to Tonta," he said a bit disappointed. I felt for him in his brief moment of dejection but I wasn't worried. I was confident everything would work out.

When he left to go to the Masjid to make Salatul Asr something unbelievable happened. As I was sitting, I felt something so strong and unexpected, I didn't know how else to describe it as anything other than inspiration from Allah. I heard an inward voice say: Just move to Tonta. I was stunned! I couldn't believe it but I was 110% certain that Allah was sending me a message. This thought didn't come from my own subconscious or my desires. It was contrary to what I wanted to do! The feeling was so unadulterated; it was as if the words were inscribed in my heart leaving me absolutely no doubt that it was the best thing to do.

I was baffled. But it doesn't make any sense, I thought to myself, trying to logically figure out the consequences of me leaving Alexandria, the place I've just gotten adjusted to, with friends, school and all to an unknown place, which I wasn't sure if I would benefit at all. But all of that meant nothing. Allah was sending me in a direction; Only He knows the future, the hidden and the unseen, so I've got to be a fool not to listen.

"Babe, you need to apologize to her," my husband told me.

"She's the one who should be apologizing to me," I demanded, "standing me up and playing games with me!"

Fajr time was approaching and my husband was on his way out to make Salah in the Masjid. I prayed, went inward and felt this humbleness come over me. Before my husband left the house I asked him to apologize to Jamillah on my behalf. He was on his way to have the first, official sit down with her and her wali to entertain the possibility of their marriage.

"Tell her I'm sorry for being snappy on the phone," I said.

He would explain to her that I'm under a lot of stress right now preparing for exams and when I kept rearranging my schedule to accommodate her and she kept putting me off, it caused me to get frustrated.

That was part of it; I didn't tell him to relay to her how her other actions really put me at disease and forever change the way I would feel about her and deal with her. For the sake of diffusing matters, I tried my best to overlook what she did but it was such a jihad. I didn't want to believe that she showing her behind on purpose but her actions made it real difficult for me to make excuses for her.

I just could not believe this was the same sweet girl that I had got to know in the beginning. Well, I guess that was the problem. I didn't really get to know who she was; I had an impression of her but I hadn't had more than two conversations with her; how much can that tell about a person? I haven't seen her in the home and I've barely had any interaction with her at all. What did I expect? This was a real eye opener, a lesson for all of eternity!

I felt this brewing animosity for her and a keen desire to give her a piece of my mind. How dare she play games, wrong me and have a nerve to be arrogant about it! Ok, I reminded myself, this is a test. I disciplined myself to overlook her faults and give her the benefit of the doubt.

But the thing that really upset me was the lack of concern Jamillah showed for my feelings, the consideration had for my time and the way she started to treat me, almost as if she was saying: "I don't need you!"

I re-visited the events in my head and tried to figure out where things turned sour. She left my apartment smiling. Then I after not hearing from her in a couple of days, she was expressing doubt and requesting to come over my house to ask me some questions. Since then, I've felt obligated to be available for her and have been adjusting my plans to accommodate her. Once she decided on perusing things with Muhammad, a couple of things happened. First, an official sit won was put into motion, where Jamillah and Muhammad would be allowed to meet and ask each other questions, with the facilitation of her wali. But there seemed to be a huge miscommunication; it seemed as if Jamillah, Muhammad and her wali all had different ideas of how things would go down and I would be left in the middle trying to facilitate any communication that could not take place between Jamillah and Muhammad and troubleshoot huge, potential problems that would arise had communication not taken place.

Firstly, she needs to take a blood test, I told Muhammad. Good thing I said something because he seemed indifferent about the issue. He agreed but he was too laidback for my liking; it was like Jamillah's wali was setting all the terms and Muhammad was just going with it, regardless of what we discussed beforehand. I understand that her wali has to play a major role and I didn't expect my opinion to be of the most significant, but if certain things weren't squared away, there was going to be major problems.

You can't make it, no problem, things happen, just have the decency to call so that I'm not waiting around for you, putting my stuff on the backburner. After altering my plans again and to accommodate her, I found myself calling her because the time she said she was going to be at my house came and left.

"I'm sorry," she whined, on the other end of the phone. I wanted to give her the benefit of the doubt but the way she said sorry did not sound sincere at all; in fact it sounded as if she was playing games. Between being under pressure during these critical moments of preparing for exams and being irritated for the lack of regard she was showing for my time, my patience had run out.

"Listen, I don't have time for this!" I blurted out. "I have things to do! I have studying to do!" I surprised myself. I hadn't intended on saying this but my feeling just took over and by the way I said it I'm sure she could tell that I was fed up. She was taken back but shortly after she responded back with an air of arrogance.

"The questions I have, you can't answer, so there's no reason for me to meet with you!" Jamillah obnoxiously said to me over the phone.

My natural instincts wanted to give her a piece of my mind. How dare she play games, and have a nerve to be haughty about it. I had to take a moment to calm my emotions. I refused to go tit for tat with her; that's the last thing I wanted and it hurt me to witness this new attitude she had towards me.

I swallowed my pride and bit my tongue. "O.K.," I said. "No problem." And we never talked since, until it was time for Muhammad to have a sit down with her and even then I didn't talk to her directly but told my husband to apologize on my behalf.

It's true, I had a chip on my shoulder. I felt bruised by Jamillah and hoped that my husband explaining to her what caused me to react the way I did, would cause her to acknowledge the grief she caused and have as much concern that I did in rectifying our relationship, so that we can have a friendly, cooperative relationship.

I guess the fact that I didn't expect her to act in the way she did really threw me for a loop. I had nothing but good expectations of her but she started to show me another side. I became deeply troubled by the situation and what had happened. For days, all I could think about was how Jamillah made me felt;I felt disregarded and disrespected. I felt this brewing animosity for her and a keen desire to make her feel the same hurt that she made me feel but I knew I couldn't allow my nafs to take over, so I resisted. I exerted all the effort that I had in me to be the bigger person; I petitioning myself to forgive her, overlook her faults and let it go. I prayed to Allah to forgive her and to make it easy for me to forgive her.

Moving mountains was easier than forgiving her and even attempting to make 70 excuses for her and think positively for her. It was a painful exertion, trying to divert my attention to other thoughts but my bruised heart kept reminding me how surprised I was that she could be so insensitive and haughty. My thoughts became consumed with what she did, what I did and what I should do better in the future. In addition, the thought of this "feud" brewing between us was causing me distress. I've heard cases about there being animosity and hatred between co-wives and this idea was always daunting. This was the one thing that I hoped I would be spared from if I was in a polygamous marriage.

There's nothing that would weigh you down more than having a spiteful relationship, especially with someone so close to home. If it works out between her and Muhammad and they have children together, their children would be siblings to my children. What kind of example would be setting if the mothers couldn't get along or if we dealt with each other with malevolence instead of kindness and respect? As the older one, the one born into the deen and the first one, I felt it was my responsibility to mend our relationship and the situation but a part of me felt like so much damage has been done. I hated the fact that we got started on the wrong foot and even if I tried my best to forgive her, I was starting to doubt whether it was possible for my heart to heal, knowing that it wasn't safe from bleeding again. I didn't feel safe around her and I couldn't figure out why. This made it even more of a struggle for me not to spend so much thought on her or the situation because I didn't have the privilege of just forgetting about her and moving on with my life. If Allah willed, she would marry my husband, therefore, making her upfront in center in my life. I spent my days amerced in prayer, asking Allah to forgive me for my shortcomings and soften my heart so I could forgive others. I re-implemented the habit of seeking Allah's forgiveness repeatedly during the day. As we know the Prophet Muhammad (SAW) sought the forgiveness of Allah 100 times a day and he had a guarantee that he would be forgiven, so who are we not to seek Allah's forgiveness frequently?

Chapter 8

"And I free not myself (from the blame). Verily, the self is inclined to evil, except when my Lord bestows His mercy. Verily, my Lord is Oft—Forgiving, Most Merciful."

I had a bitter taste in my mouth about what happened between me and Jamillah and I hoped we would be able to patch things up and continue to build our relationship as sisters in Islam, regardless what happened with her and my husband.

Muhammad came home from the sit-down telling me about a contract between them that would take place the following week. I went off on him. This isn't what we agreed on. What happened to her taking a blood test and where would she live. You didn't get the other place in Tonta yet, I reminded him. What will that mean, until I moved to Tonta, she would be hanging out at our apartment. She already had a way of pushing my buttons, I could imagine her showing up at our home and doing all types of stuff to get under my skin. I was getting agitated by the minute thinking about everything that was taking place and seeing where things were going. My husband was not a passive person but he was just allowing Jamillah's wali to dictate everything that would take place without speaking up. I wasn't going for it. I made it clear that I was not happy with the way things were going and I wasn't budging on the two main issues: her taking a blood test before the marriage and him getting the place in Tonta and me being able to comfortably move in without being pressured to leave because of someone else's anxiousness to move in.

Muhammad quietly listened to me and then called her wali to tell him that he will not marry her until he gets the place in Tonta. I had to go to the bathroom to cool off. I hadn't remember feeling anger like that in a long, long time. I cannot believe I allowed shaytan to get me like that and hadn't realized how much emotions I was feeling: rage, hurt, anxiousness and most of all fear. I was afraid that me and my husband's marriage would go downhill from this point onwards and that we may not even survive. What's more, I feared that Jamillah would bring out the worse in me and cause me to end up lashing out on her because of her immature and insensitive behavior. What did I get myself into, I thought. I did *not* see this coming! My husband was making plans to marry this other woman and the dynamics of our marriage would change forever.

"Could you ask your husband to come to my house because I have another question to ask him," Jamillah said with an attitude. Excuse me?! This girl really has some nerve, I thought to myself. This was the first time we spoke since the episode over the phone and she didn't feel compelled to excuse herself for her past actions or even acknowledge the message I sent to her with my husband. In fact, she showed no concern to clear up any possible misunderstanding or neutralize the "bad blood" that was thickening between us. But after not talking to each other for at least a week, the news of Muhammad delaying marrying her motivated her to call me right away and request another meeting with him and her wali at her house again.

Her proud attitude and lack of regard for her actions intensified the animosity and overwhelming distaste I had for her and her character. It just made even more convinced that she didn't have concern for me or my feelings.

I took a moment to compose myself. "He's not home right now but I'll call him and ask if he can meet you tomorrow," I calmly told the sister.

Then after calling him and confirming that he could do it, I called her back to give her the time he was available. "He can meet you after shuruq."

"What?!" she asked with conceit, clearly not knowing what the word shuruq meant.

"About an hour or so after Fajr."

And that was it. She had nothing else to say.

But as Allah would have it, the plans of her mother would put a monkey wrench in her desire to meet right away. A couple of minutes later I got another phone call from Jamillah. Though the previous times I talked to her, her attitude sucked, I did not prevent me from dealing with her in the same courteous manner that I've been treating her in the beginning. I gave her the proper greeting, salaming her as if I were salaaming a friend who I was happy to hear from and she responded like an immature school girl, horridly saying "Walaikum Assalam" and then getting straight to business.

Every time she called, I tried it again.

"Assalamualaikum," I answered the phone pleasantly.

Her voice resembled that of one humbled.

"How are you?" I asked, following the same protocol I did when talking to any of my sisters.

"I'm fine," she said. "How are you?"

"Alhumdulillah," I answered.

"My mother and her husband are going to Cairo tomorrow so were not going to be able to meet," she said. Look at that, I thought to myself.

Then for the next couple of minutes she was trying to devise a plan so that she can meet with me and Muhammad.

"I don't know if you think it's appropriate or not but maybe I can come to your house?" she asked humbly.

I got straight to the point. "What's this about, the marriage contract?"

She hesitated. "Uh, yeah. I thought it was going to be next week," she said, clearly anxious about getting married to my husband.

"I'll ask him when he gets in and well get back to you."

I thought back to when she was in my apartment and she briefly told me about her co-wife who came to her house with some sisters shortly after she married her husband. From the way she told the story, her husband's first wife was the aggressor but I thought about the way she was provoking me and could have imagined what was the case for the sister who was married to the brother who Allah knows how long? I agreed with her marrying

Muhammad in the beginning and she didn't even marry my husband and I was already battling my emotions and my nafs, who knows what kind of drama that sister went through. It doesn't justify the first wife coming to her house and starting drama, if in face she did that but if she kept provoking me the way she did, especially after marrying my husband, I would be tempted to give her a beat down too.

There were certain things I would not tolerate. I would not tolerate coming to my house unannounced and I would not tolerate her making demands to see her husband and refusing to leave when announced. Of course she didn't do that and they weren't even married yet but I could predict her doing all kinds of things to get attention. She already admitted that she was jealous and insecure but I didn't think much of it because we all feel jealousy once in a while but there is a difference between feeling jealousy and seeking refuge in Allah and making an effort to not act on it and being a jealousy and insecure person who doesn't strive against it and uphold a high standard of character.

I think now I figured out why she said she loved polygamy. I'm pretty sure if she was the first wife she wouldn't have such enthusiasm to be down with it. You see if she's jealousy and insecure, there's a lack of confidence that she would maintain her husband's interest and love. But if she comes in as second, hoping to grab her husband's attention when things are bland between him and his first wife, then she becomes the prized possession. I guess she assumed that because Muhammad was getting a second wife, the fire was gone between us and she could come in, steal his love and throw it in my face. But little did she know, me and my husband were more than just husband and wife, we were friends.

When Muhammad came home from work, I was disturbed, withdrawn and unable to give him a smile or ask him about his day. Without him even having to inquire what was wrong, he picked up on my being perturbed and began to feel for me. He's been noticing what the situation was doing to me lately and he was not happy about that.

I was trying so hard not to be consumed by emotions but it was having a toll on me. I found myself so mentally exhausted that I wasn't compelled to engage in cheery dialogue and I didn't want to be bothered at all. Almost everything that I did, my mind was absent, when I cooked or clean, I wasn't really there and when I fed my daughter or took care of her, I was just going through the motions. It was hard to fully devote myself to any task because I was so troubled by the recent events.

I sat down and grabbed a paper and pen. My husband knew what that meant; I was troubled and need to write to express myself and find remedy. When I felt clogged, I secluded myself from everyone and everything in my life, attempted to go inward and resolve whatever emotions I was feeling. Seeing me in that state bothered him so he picked up a paper and pen also.

"I'm going to write the sister a letter," he said and in a brief letter, he told her very firmly, there's no need to rush getting married because there's some things that need to get ironed out. First, she has to get a blood test. Then he admonished her, saying if it's her intention to test, he's advising her not to because she's not qualified to do so and ended it off by asking her: "please don't turn this into a burden."

He read the letter to me, from start to finish and once he got my approval, sent it to her little brother who would give it to her. I felt good about what he did; he showed a true concern for my feelings and he was stepping up and making sure the things we agreed on would be implemented for the betterment of all parties involved. I felt confident that if he practiced polygamy he would do it the right way. It wasn't him I was worried about, it was the fitna of the incoming party that kept me up at night.

Jamillah wouldn't let up. As soon as she received the letter from my husband, she was now passing messages on to her brother to tell Muhammad that she wanted to meet. I was starting to get tired of hearing her name; every time you turn around there was something else. She was stressing to meet as if it was urgent and at the rate she wanted to meet, it didn't seem as if she had much to do with her time, almost as if she wanted everyone to drop everything because she wants to meet. The demands in my life were constantly tugging on me; I had no time to waste on petty stuff that would threaten my peace of mind even further. I was married, had a baby, was in school and tried to memorize the Qur'an in my spare time. I saw her as impeding on my time and space and wish she'd take it easy. I understood she wanted to get married badly but she didn't realize what this was doing to me; this was a huge adjustment for me and I didn't want to feel like I was being cornered and forced to deal with this when I wasn't emotionally steady. I felt like I was this close to letting Jamillah have it and I didn't want to have to go there with her. It took all the discipline in the world to restrain myself from lashing out on her and dealing with her in the same respectful manner that I do everyone else, regardless of how much she irritated me. I kept praying for her and kept fighting against my nafs and felt stronger and more connected to Allah, each time.

"I can meet with her after I finish with my exams," I told my husband, "so if she really wants to meet with me, then she'll have to wait."

I learned my lesson. I was done breaking my neck to accommodate her; it was crunch time and if I didn't zero in on my studies, I would only have myself to blame. Besides, something told me that she wasn't interested in meeting with me anyway; after getting that letter I'm sure her concern was clearing her name with Muhammad, after all he did hit her pretty hard in the letter. And if it involved meeting with me too, being that she's not going to meet with him alone, all right, but something told me chatting with me wasn't at the top of her priority list. After all, how much time did she have to reach out to me before the letter incident, yet all she could talk to me about was wanting to meet my husband. But still, I gave her the benefit of the doubt, after all only Allah knows our true intentions and only he knows our hearts.

I was friends with Jamillah's mother; she was a nice sister who friendly and easy to talk with. I called her and Jamillah happened to pick up. "What are you doing today?" Jamillah asked nonchalantly as if we were buddies.

"I have some business to take care of," I said dryly. She had to know that I wasn't going to just drop everything and meet her on demand like that, not anymore.

Then I offered clemency and initiated meeting with her, without her even having to ask. It was obvious she wanted to talk; I wasn't going to make it harder on her. After eating a little humble pie, I Imagined her reflecting and learning her lesson by now.

"I'm pretty busy but I'm available Monday if you want to meet."

"What time?" she asked.

"How about the morning?" I knew she usually didn't get her day started until the afternoon but with all of my demands, the best thing for me was to get it over with and get my day started.

"What time in the morning," she asked inquisitively. From the way she said it, I knew she wasn't enthusiastic about meeting early in the morning. Of course she had been motivated to meet my husband because that was the best time he could meet, but if she had a choice, if she didn't have to get out of bed so early, she didn't.

I let out a friendly laugh and Jamillah joined in with me. We ended on a good note. It seems like things were off to a better start. I was happy about that. I was willing to compromise. I knew she wasn't a morning person.

"I tell you what, we'll confirm beforehand and decide on a time."

I got off the phone feeling light. Maybe I had her all wrong, I thought. I'm willing to give her a second chance and start on a clean slate. But the events that would take place the next couple of days would have me on emotional roller coaster and have wondering what I got myself into.

I was crying in my Salah thanking Allah for delaying my husband marrying her. In wake of Muhammad taking the initiative to meet with Jamillah to see why she wanted to meet so badly, he came back with information that I wasn't ready to hear. I couldn't believe what she said out of her mouth to my husband. The more I got to know her, I more I realized she was nothing how I perceived her to be. I wasn't so sure I wanted her marrying my husband anymore and if so, I didn't know how long our marriage would survive. I was shocked and terribly disgusted at what I learned. What was her intention in wanting to meet? Was it so she could get him to feel sorry for her, manipulate him and convince him to marry her sooner than later? I didn't want to believe that but I couldn't figure out why she told him what she did. Muhammad having the kind nature that he did, didn't suspect that she was trying to manipulate him or anything like that and I didn't even tell him of my qualms but instead, kept calculating everything and it didn't add up. Something wasn't right.

That was the longest and most passion-filled Salah I ever recall making; I just cried out to Allah hysterically, unable to stop while reciting the Surahs to myself and I didn't even try to stop, being well aware that there was nothing wrong with it. If anything, this was a praised act, we don't need to hold back tears from Allah. I couldn't show my gratitude enough to Allah. Thank you, Allah! Thank you!

I managed to re-focus and get my last bit of studying in for exams. I was still bothered about the recent information I learned and the whole situation in general but I continued to pray and do my best to stay on task. Once I finished taking my exams, I exhaled and was able to relax a little bit more.

"Tell Jamillah if she still wants to meet tomorrow, she can come at 12:00. If she doesn't want to meet anymore, it's o.k. just ask her to give me a call and let me know so that I'm not waiting for her. Sometimes I have to leave the house and make errands," I told her little brother.

It was the day before Monday, the day that we agreed on when she answered her mother's phone. But now that she already met with Muhammad and they were back on good terms again, I wasn't so sure if she was still interested in meeting with me anymore.

"Allah, please send me a sign if she's sincere or not. If she's not sincere, don't send her to my house today," I prayed.

The appointed time came. It was Monday at 12:00 and no sign of Jamillah. Maybe, she woke up late, I thought to myself. I'll give her respite. I continued to take care of things I needed to get done in the house. I wasn't bothered at all. I purposely picked a day where I wouldn't have to take care of any urgent matters out of the house and since I was finished studying for my exams, I wouldn't be annoyed because I wasn't allowing her to rob precious, studying time from me anymore. I looked at the time from time to time but I never stopped what I was doing. I remained focused on taking care of what I had to take care of as if I hadn't expected a visitor. I learned my lesson; I wasn't going to call her or anything. It was asked that she show courtesy, but if she doesn't feel a need to, then that's between her and Allah. At a certain time, I stopped checking the time all together and instead of getting irritated like I did in the past; I was quite happy. I was jubilant with the idea of not allowing her or the situation to stress me anymore; I was taking on way too much and it wasn't healthy for me. The idea of it being dissolved put me at ease. I was mentally exhausted! It was time for me to move on with my life. It was 10 p.m. and Jamillah never came to my house and she didn't call to excuse herself or give any explanations. I never called her and went to bed feeling at rest.

"Assalamualaikum, is Jamillah awake?" I asked her mother on the phone, the next day.

"No, she's still sleeping."

"It's o.k., you don't have to wake her. I have a gift for her. I'll just leave it for her."

"Did you give Jamillah the message?" I asked Jamillah's brother. "Did you ask her to call me and let me know if she can't make it?"

"Yes," he said.

"O.K., I just wanted to confirm you got the message."

I gave him the gift; it was a notebook with a note in it encouraging her not to give up. I told her that I find writing very helpful and I urged her to write her feelings and experiences as well as a means of therapy. I happily signed it: your sister in Islam. I had intended to give her the gift when she came to my home, so I figured I'd give it to her now.

In addition, she got another surprise; it was a letter from my husband. Inside the letter, it said: "I can't marry you."

Within a couple of minutes after giving the notebook and the letter to her brother, Jamillah was calling my phone. I didn't answer.

My husband and I had a day of fun and fish. He took me to visit some friends and we celebrated moving on with our marriage without the extra baggage. Yes, it was official; he broke off all ties with the sister and from that day on our relationship improved, even better than before Jamillah was in the picture. Allah is so Akbar!

Chapter 9

"Surely, your Lord is Allah who created the heavens and the earth in six days and then istawa (rose above) the throne (in a matter that suits His majesty), disposing the affairs of all things. No intercessor (can plead with Him) except after His leave. That is Allah, your Lord; so worship Him (alone). Then will you not remember?" (10: 3)

Moving to Tonta was an exciting experience! I looked forward to the new change, new town, meeting new friends and new experiences. I spent most of the two hour plus train ride, looking out the window, appreciating Allah's beautiful creation. I didn't have a school lined up yet, but I would just have to be patient. Allah blessed me to attend there; He can replace me with something better, easily.

I visited the wife of one of Muhammad's friends. She was the one of the few African Americans I met since coming to Egypt. She was real down to earth, funny and easy to talk with. She welcomed me in her home and had me laughing without even making much of an effort to do so. At her house there was another sister there who happened to be doing her daughter's hair. She was also cool too and had a warm spirit about her. I could tell by the way they joked and interacted, they were real good friends.

"I breast fed all of them," my host said proudly, referring to her co-wife's children.

The sister who was doing her daughter's hair was her co-wife and they had the most cheerful and easy-going friendship ever. They happily co-existed and helped each other on a daily basis. After one gave birth, the other cooked for her and after one had surgery, the other gave up her days with her husband so that he could assist her as it was difficult for her to bathe and apply bandages by herself.

I thought that was the coolest thing! My heart melted. This is the type of relationship I envisioned having with my co-wife if I were to be in polygamy and being that things were going in the opposite direction, I continuously thanked Allah for sparing me from being in such a strenuous situation. Though I was willing to take part in a polygamous marriage, Allah knows what each of us can and can't handle. I just thank Him for allowing me to learn the lesson without being put through the ringer. Still my negative experience did not make me view polygamy in a deleterious way. Polygamy itself has many benefits but some people are not mature enough to take part in it and thus they tarnish the idea of two or more people being married to the same man.

I was so proud by the maturity, compassion and respect exhibited by my two new friends. They had different personalities but I loved them and appreciated them for who they are, just as their husband has been able to do. He had it down to a science because he followed the Sunnah of Prophet Muhmmad (SAW). He housed them in separate quarters; one lived in an apartment downstairs and another lived right upstairs. There was a constant revolving door of their children visiting one another and some of them attending class together. The husband spent two days at one's house and two days at another's house and gave each of them the respect of not mentioning the other one, talking about the other one or seeing the other one who's turn it wasn't.

"Me or my co-wife don't know where my husband's heart lies. When he's with me, he's with me and when he's with her, he's with her."

I smiled. "May Allah continue to bless you guys," I told her. I realized the way the husband dealt with and treated his wives were key. Being that the women are in such a vulnerable state, what the husband did or didn't do could make the difference between night and day. He could be fueling enmity and jealousy between them without even knowing it. Naturally both wives would want to be the one more beloved to the husband and by him showing more affection to one or showing more enthusiasm to be with one or casting another to the side could not only affect the wife's self-esteem but cause them to breed feelings of resentment, jealousy and hatred to her co-wife. Polygamy is no walk in the park; it's a very delicate situation and all parties must be qualified to deal with it. Sometimes the man thinks he is capable of handling it but in the process ruins both marriages and leaves a bad taste in the children's mouths; in some cases it can be so destructive that the impression that they get from their parent's marriage affects them for life. Look what happened to me.

If marriage between two people takes work, those involved in a plural marriage better be prepared to roll up their sleeves. But it can be done and seeing the beautiful way my two new friends were able to work together peacefully without the drama, jealousy or spite made me feel good knowing there are people out there who are benefitting from something that Allah has allowed for a reason. Women continue to outnumber men and with things such as a high number of male incarceration rate, especially in the Black community, polygamy facilitates many women to get married, who would otherwise have the option of being alone for the rest of their lives or do something many women in the West would admit to: taking matters in their own hands by having an affair with a man already taken or attempt to take him away from his spouse. The stealth of this when compared to the honesty of a legitimate marriage to more than one woman and children who are not bastards and unaccounted for, makes polygamy seem more advantageous. Still, anyone who rushes into polygamy without having the discipline and without thinking it through and planning may cause more devastation than good. It is a serious decision that should propel one to be very honest with themselves about their capabilities before delving into and a matter that must be taken with care.

Some would have imagined the drama taking place between me and the sister who almost married my husband to affect our relationship in a negative way but Allah can make all things happened. It was a gift from Allah because He caused to bring me and my husband closer together. Being in that situation tested our relationship and caused it to become stronger. It was during that time when he was planning to marry her that caused him to share something with me that he never did before; Allah guided him to be honest with me and completely open up the doors of communication to a whole other lever. As a result our relationship improved in a multitude of ways in addition to our appreciation for one another.

We spent more quality time together and at one point I was actually looking forward to when he came home. He ate, shared with me any interesting or funny events of the day and we just talked. I enjoyed his company and his peculiar sense of humor. From the serious impression that people got of him, no one would have ever guessed how much he made me laughed in the home. And he was able to do it without even trying; since he knew me so well, it was easy for him to know what tickled me. I really believed he enjoyed making me have a good laugh; there were times when I was on the floor from uncontrollable laughter and he continued to crack me up.

There was nothing so valuable than having a mate who knew me so well and cared enough to consider my emotions. When he saw I was disturbed, annoyed, or upset, he would stop everything and try everything to comfort me and wouldn't leave me until he saw a smile. I really appreciated that; this showed me that there wasn't anything worth doing if his wife wasn't o.k. Making sure his other half was stable and there was peace in the home was a priority to him. This held a great weight with me and softened my heart a great deal when my heart was in need of it most.

Muhammad and I virtually stopped arguing. I learned to be patient and listen to him, without cutting him off, though at times I did slip when I really wanted to get my point across. Still, the times I was convinced I was right, I had a new attitude. I sincerely tried to look at the situation so that we could come to a resolution. This felt much better than trying to battle him and over-speak him, only to feel guilty at the end. Now, I was able to not get too upset because I was beginning to look at the bigger picture. So what if I lose an argument, that's much easier than losing my husband's home. And what's the point of being right if you're not happy. In time I learned that me being fierce with my husband and trying to get him to see my point wasn't wise; it was exhausting, time-consuming and it brought little good, if any at all. I began to enjoy taking a chill pill, being humble and listening more. Maybe there was a misunderstanding somewhere. Maybe if I listened more and talked less, I can see where there was a breakdown in communication. In addition, I began to view the way I serve my husband in a different light. I recalled a time when I would delay praying Esha up until my husband came home so I would have an excuse from serving his dinner or giving him something to drink. I knew that he wasn't going to wait until I finished praying to ask me to serve him as some husbands do who "can't do anything in the kitchen." He would just fix his own meal and make his own tea, thereby relieving me from feeling like the "slave" who has to do something. Later on I realized how horrible this way of me. I was only shortchanging my own self by losing out on the blessings but being at the place where I was, no one could have convinced me of this. It was something I had to learn on my own and by struggling against my nafs, changing the way I thought and by praying a lot, in time I began to become much happier with myself, my husband and my life and felt at peace. Before I couldn't understand the significance of women going to the kitchen to get something for their husbands, when they could get it themselves, but in time I got the answer. I know knew why.

Chapter 10

"You are only a warner." (35:23)

"Abdul Hakim's getting married today!" my husband alerted me in alarm over the phone.

"Are you serious?!"

"Yeah, I'm trying to call him but I can't get in contact with him," Muhammad said anxiously.

There was nothing I could do but I felt flattered that he chose to call me to seek comfort. After all, I *was* his friend.

He was concerned about Abdul Hakim's welfare. He was going to marry Jamillah, the same girl he almost married. Abdul Hakim came to Muhammad only a couple of days prior because he was warned about marrying the sister. He inquired my husband about it, knowing that he almost was going to marry her. In a very vague way, without exposing the sister's dirty laundry, Muhammad strongly advised his friend against marrying her, simply asking him if he wants to be married to someone who is dishonest. Still, the brother needed details and once he saw my husband wasn't going to say much more, he stopped. "She should tell you," Muhammad said.

Then he advised him to speak to Yasin, another brother she almost married but didn't go through because of fitna that she initiated between her and his wife, who had opened her arms to her and welcomed her even after she sent hints that she was interested in her husband. In fact, it was due to Yasin's wife telling her that she didn't mind her marrying her husband that her husband even considered taking her as a second wife. Once Yasin witnessed the behavior of Jamillah, he cut the ties with her before even having a sit down.

"Did Abdul Hakim talk to you like I told him to do? My husband asked Yasin.

"No," Yasin responded.

Instead of taking the advice of someone who knew the sister and doing a background check, he proceeded to marry the girl, without inviting Muhammad or Omar to the wedding. Abdul Hakim already had two wives and the information that he didn't know about her could not only jeopardize his health but his wives as well.

It was only hours until the wedding would take place. Muhammad kept trying to reach Abdul Hakim until he finally got through.

"Listen, did the sister tell you about her condition?" My husband asked her.

"No," Abdul Hakim said, clueless.

"She has a disease and it's not curable."

"I'll call you back," Abdul Hakim said, hurrying off the phone.

Only Allah knows what conversation took place between Abdul Hakim and Jamillah but the next day Abdul Hakim no longer looked at Muhammad in the same friendly way that he always did but stood with his arms folded, sizing him up. He looked at him suspiciously as if he was trying to discern the truth.

"What's this about this disease?"

"We're talking about a STD here," Muhammad told him.

Abdul Hakim wanted to know exactly what it was but Muhammad didn't want to reveal any of the sister's faults. But when it became clear that he wasn't letting up, he gave in.

"What is it?"

When husband finally told him the STD that his wife had, he nearly lost his mind.

"I seek refuge in Allah from the evil of shaytan!" the brother screamed out in distressed.

It was too late. He already married her, on the same day my husband called him to give him the news about her condition.

"I hate to be the bearer of bad news," Muhammad said compassionately. "Let me know if you need anything?"

It was nothing like seeing up close and personal the disaster that would have befallen me and my husband had not Allah showered his grace upon us and exposed the sister before Muhammad made the commitment of marrying her. He was this close to being persuaded into marrying her right away and this close to doing it without having taken a blood test.

"Marriage is something you're not supposed to delay," I recall the brothers telling my husband, in effort to get him to marry the girl right away.

This may be the case but a polygamous situation is something you have to plan for and if you fail to do so, the results can be disastrous. Look at this case here. Not only did the brother jeopardize himself but he jeopardized the women who he was married to because of haste and a stubbornness in doing what he wanted despite the signs sent to him.

Chapter 11

"Or think you that you will enter Paradise without such (trials) as came to those who passed away before you? They were afflicted with severe Poverty, Ailments & were Shaken". (Quran 2:214)

The riots in Egypt spread and the instability of the government declined along with the order and stability of the country. My family was alarmed! The fear that my parents would never see their daughter and their granddaughter, who they never saw before, became more ostensible. My parents doubled teamed me and called me from the States to petition us to come back but we couldn't even if we wanted to. The baby didn't have her passport and due to the conditions the U.S. Embassy was shut down. It was reported that all Americans were highly encouraged to leave the country. Almost every time you turned around, we heard of more Americans returning back to the U.S., even those Muslim Americans who intended to make Hijrah and adopt Egypt as their new home, as we did. But as the conditions became more and more serious, we realized the importance, now so even more than ever, to establish and maintain a deep connection with Allah; for only our Lord could foresee what was ahead and grant us the protection and guidance we so desperately needed.

My baby hadn't even made it to her first year before I found myself pregnant *again*. Allah's the best of the planners I reminded myself, trying to see the silver lining. I felt exhausted, overwhelmed and fragile as ever but still I tried to push through with every effort to make it day by day. I couldn't find a steady flow in taking care of my baby, managing the house, cleaning and million and one chores that came in between, not to mention trying to attend to the needs of my husband, *forget it*. The spontaneity was sucked out of my life and I was deprived of the ability to going here and there, by myself, as I was pleased. Due to the instability of the country, we needed to take security measures and it wasn't safe for me to go out with the baby alone. I understood this was necessary for me and the baby's security but I *hated* it. I felt inhibited and I had nothing to look forward to; I still wasn't able to find a school yet to give me something purposeful outside of the mundane housework, in addition to aiding my mind with the mental stimulation and challenge it needed to thrive. Muhammad's day at work became increasingly longer which limited the help he could offer in the house. Still he incorporated it in his routine to help me as much as he could. Before he left for work he took the baby out of the crib and put her in a make-shift crib he had set up in the front room, near the window. This way, the baby would be getting vitamin D, something that the doctor pointed out that she lacked. If it wasn't for my husband doing this practice, my poor daughter would have stayed there in the crib, deprived of sunlight and food because by the time I woke up I was so backed up with a list of things to do and had no idea where to start. By the time I fully woke up, I had to make sure I make Salatul Zhur before it went out, eat to give myself some energy, have some food prepared for my husband to take with him to work, make sure his outfit was ironed if it wasn't already and be available to assist him in getting out the house, if needed.

I became increasingly guilty for not making breakfast for my husband in the morning. Most of the times by the time I woke up, usually late in the afternoon, he had already eaten, fed the baby and was on his way out the door for work. On some occasions, I attempted to assist him in getting things ready for work, but waking up in a state of confusion and bewilderment and not knowing where to start, left me severely limited in assisting him, my baby and even myself for that matter.

"Do I have any clothes?" Muhammad asked.

It took me a while to recollect my thoughts and understand what he was asking.

I hit my forehead with the palm of my hand. He was getting ready for work and I had forgotten to iron his clothes again.

"That's all right, he said calmly, looking through the closet for the least wrinkled outfit to wear. How many times does he have to do this before you get it together, I asked myself, beating up on myself. I didn't have a system for keeping up with his clothes, the chores or the baby and I didn't have a clue on how to develop one. I intended to get it all done, telling myself: today is going to be better. But the moment things fell apart, I retreated, feeling disappointed and frustrated. I felt like a failure to myself and my husband, not to mention my daughter who got her needs met only when I had the ability to dig deep for the strength and will power. I had no activities for her, I wasn't talking to her, reading to her or encouraging her to crawl or pull up on the crib. She, like her mother, soon became lifeless, just sitting in the crib, with nothing much to look forward to. How can I have another child? I can barely take care of this one. What will happen to me after I have this baby, I worried inwardly. Yes, it definitely was a blessing but I wanted to make sure I was in a state where I could receive it as such. I was in turmoil and didn't know where to turn. I continued praying to Allah; I knew He had the answers; I just had to be patient.

"Are you going to welcome your new neighbor?" my husband asked me.

I paused for a moment. No one moved into the building except his friend, Abdul Hakim, who was accompanied with his new wife, Jamillah.

As we know, the Prophet Muhammad (SAW) stressed kind treatment to your neighbors and relayed to us the astronomical rewards for having such conduct. I had become more accustomed to offering food and treats to neighbors and trying to show as much acts of kindness as I could to them and really enjoyed it. I had a good relationship with *all* of my neighbors and it was always an exchange of good vibes and mutual well-wishing.

However, my interactions with Jamillah have had the opposite effect. She was known to start fitna, even with those who treat her kindly. I learned that a lot of people were angry with her and it seemed as if she wasn't the least bit concerned at all; if I didn't know any better I would have thought she had a disease-of the heart-because her actions testified that she enjoyed hurting people and doing everything she could to get under people's skin.

I forgave Jamillah but have always used caution being around her because I wasn't sure of what she was capable of; I didn't quite trust her and I wasn't sure if it was wise to be around her at all. A part of me thought maybe I should just leave where we left off on a good note rather than risk bad blood being bolt once again.

"Good can only come from good," my husband would say. His philosophy was you can't lose by being kind, regardless of the results or response from others. I agreed to a certain extent. I was the type who kept my distance unless I was absolutely sure that the other side would respond positively. Otherwise, if I got any inkling that someone didn't want to be bothered, I won't even make the attempt to approach them, even if there was a possibility of good coming from it. However, my husband challenged me to get out of my box and open myself up to more blessings. I always thought he had a purer heart than mine. He was able to turn the other check and be good to the same person who wronged him without even thinking about it. On the other hand, for me it was a process! It took hard work and much effort! Alhumdulillah, I was willing to go through it because I knew it was beneficial but I was always careful about not putting myself in a position where I could get hurt. Even if it involves good, if there is a possibility of me feeling slighted and getting hurt, that was a big deal and I had to think about if it was worth it. My husband was the type that would profit by staking up his scale of blessings by partaking in the same good deeds that people like me gave up by sitting there thinking about it.

"This is a race for good deeds," he would remind me but with me and my stubborn ways, it took a while for this concept to sink in. But once I was willing to take the risk of stepping out there and imparting kindness on others without allowing the fear of people's response interfere, it has proved to be the most phenomenal experience for me.

I just wasn't sure if it was the wise thing to do in this situation. I wanted to believe that Jamillah has grown since the experience but I had to be prepared that she was the same person with the same ways. I just wanted to protect myself from any possible harm and avoid any possible fitna.

Not long after my husband cut ties with her, when we were still living in Alex, I saw her at the Masjid. This was only a few weeks after she stood me up and I sent the notebook and letter from my husband to her. At that moment when she saw me face to face, I sensed her tenseness in not knowing how to respond or react to me. She had attempted to call my phone but I didn't answer and she had no idea why. For all she knew, I could have been pissed at her and was waiting to see her in person so I could roast her or embarrass her in front of everyone. Would I put her on the hot seat and question her about what happened, causing her to search for excuses or stutter. Would I expose her faults to everyone and rally everyone to turn against her?

Although I was tempted to question her about the last incident, I decided against it. I didn't expose her faults, embarrass her and made no attempt to rally the people against her or even broadcast that she harmed me. I refrained from putting her in the hot seat or even bringing up the incident at all.

Instead, I embraced her with a big hug and offered her the salams. I asked her how she was and continued on my path. I knew I made the right decision. It felt good choosing the higher road and I was confident that Allah would repay me by giving me more than a brief satisfaction of seeing her swarm. It was over and I was able to forgive her and move on with my life.

Jamillah opened the door, seemingly happy to see my face.

"I'm not going to stay. I just wanted to give you this," I told her. It was a plate of chicken stew. She thanked me and I was on my way. That was easy, I thought to myself. Kindness doesn't cost anything but it's the most needed thing in the world; it softens hearts and inspires others to confer the same kindness upon others. Sometimes the person least deserving of kindness is in need of it the most.

Something astounding happened when I came back to my apartment. The lethargic and dead feeling I had previous to the trip had disappeared. I now felt light and happy. This act of kindness not only helped my neighbor but it helped me. I couldn't believe how such a small act could impact me in such a huge way. By simply doing a selfless act for someone else, without expecting anything in return, I was benefitting from it as well. The good response that I got for her and lack of fitna encouraged me to increase doing in seeking good deeds. This didn't mean I was suddenly her best friend. I didn't visit her every day, but was just conscious of looking out for her and helping her in any way that I could. I learned that I could develop a relationship with her without getting to close, thereby protecting myself from any possible harm. I gave her the benefit of the doubt but I didn't put myself in a position where I would be vulnerable to her or receiving harm from her. I never told her my business, never asked her for anything and I was the one who came to her house to drop off items, she didn't come to mine. In time, she began to feel more comfortable with me and I even noticed her beginning to offer to share food with me. This shocked me and since I never expected her to return any favors to me, I wasn't excited about this. However, I was beginning to see that maybe Allah was using me as an example to her and who knows maybe she had turned a new leaf. If so, who knows of the enormous rewards credited to me for being patient with her and daring to deal with her with rahma.

The elated feeling I got being nice to Jamillah was wholesome, but it was going to take more than a couple of acts of kindness to transform my condition. I was in a whole. I had to convince myself to get out of bed each day, and when I was up, I dragged my feet to take care of things, with lost hope that the day would be any better than the previous ones. I failed in keeping the house tidy, in taking care of the baby sufficiently and taking care of myself. I walked around with dumpy clothes, undone hair and no desire to do better. I just accepted that things would continue to roll over to the next day and made no real effort to getting them under control.

I fell into severe depression. I woke up later and later, and only got up when it was time to make Salah. I struggled against my nafs to get up but Alhumdulillah, I was able to make my Salahs. I was tempted to fall back in and but if it wasn't for my baby I probably would have. Your baby needs you, I told myself, myself to exert discipline in at least preparing food for her and myself. Then I had to wash her, change her and be there for her but with no motivation to live life, this meant exerting twice the effort. I knew she needed more. She needed her mother but mentally I wasn't there.

Just making wudu exerted so much effort. O.K., you can do it, I convinced myself and made myself go through with the necessary rituals until the next time. Knowing that prayer was beneficial for me, especially during this time was the only thing that got me through.

I sat there on the bathroom stall for almost a half an hour, twisting my hair, thinking, praying for strength and trying to convince myself to get up so I can take care of what I have to take care of. But it was hard to level with myself. It's not like I could tell myself, just take care of these things and then you can do what you want to do. I knew that would never be the case. No matter how much I tried, I would always be behind schedule and would always be left doing things that I have to do and never having any time for the things I want to do. Life became a barrage of never-ending responsibilities and monotonous, boring-filled days.

I wanted to die but wasn't senseless enough to even attempt taking my life. I knew I was suffering now, I didn't want to be dragged to Hell and be condemned to the raging fire for eternity.

"Allah doesn't give us more than we can handle," I reminded myself. "Allah is with the patient."

O.K., I told myself, just be patient, this will pass. But my condition got worse. I knew if I didn't get help soon not only would my baby suffer but my unborn child, growing inside of me would really suffer. I didn't want anyone to worry about me but I knew it wasn't wise for me to stay in that state until the point of no return. Then people would really worry about me.

Chapter 12

"See you not that Allah sends down water from the sky and we produce therewith fruits of various colors and among the mountains and streaks white and red, of various colors and (others) very black." (Qur'an 35:27)

"You need to come home baby," my step mother said. I knew she would say that.

My husband didn't agree. According to him, we were home. He thought I should seek help there first. I knew there were deep rooted issues that had to be addressed and wasn't so sure anyone in Egypt could help me. Also, staying there, where I didn't have the support I needed was futile. In Egypt, people were basically connected with their families; your parents, sisters and brothers were ready to assist you in any way you needed. Of course there were exceptional people like Um Osama who reached out to ex-bats in the community like me but other than that, you're basically on your own. I dreamed of going back home and seeing my family again; it had been almost three years since I've seen my mother, father, sisters and brothers, and other relatives. I knew they would embrace this baby and the new one on the way and support me and help me find my way. My husband was great but there was only so much he could do and with my growing needs I was starting to feel more and more like a burden on him.

My husband told me if I went back to the States it would make my condition worse and my step mother told me the opposite. I needed to sit down, think things through and hear my own voice. Muhammad already made it clear that he wasn't going with me and if I decided to go, I would be on my own. He had a feeling that if I left, it would be the last time we saw each other and that somehow this may be the lead to my demise. This scared me; I knew he didn't know the future but he was pretty wise and on point with many of the things that he said in the past. On the other hand, my condition was steadily deteriorating and I had the responsibility of taking care of my children and at the rate I was going I would be taking my children downhill with me.

I cleared all the thoughts from my head. I forgot about what everyone wanted for and sought the counsel of the most important one in my life, my Lord. I made Salatul Istikharah, then I patiently waited for the answer. Within a couple of days I felt a strong feeling in my heart, the same one that I did which let me know moving to Tonta was the right thing to do.

I knew my husband wasn't going to be pleased but we only please our husbands in order to please our Lord.

"I made my decision," I told my husband. "I'm going."

He immediately made plans for us to go to the U.S. Embassy. When we went there, something amazing happened. Not only did the entire process go through smoothly but we were able to get it expedited quickly, giving me and the baby the green light to fly right away. Allahu Akbar. Not only that but something happened that sent shock waves throughout my body. Allah showed me how he could change someone's heart, just like that.

"You know," my husband said. "Now I think it's a good idea for you two to go."

I could hardly believe the words that were coming out of his words.

I never thought he would agree to us leaving and here he was confessing that he preferred my decision above his! Allah is so Akbar!

The next thing you know, we were in the car on our way to the airport. We left the house hours before the departure time but found ourselves trapped in traffic. The driver wasn't moving fast enough for me; it was almost as if he forgot that we had a flight to catch.

"Tell him to hurry up!" I ordered my husband. "I'm going to miss my flight."

If we didn't make it there soon, we were going to miss our flight. I looked at the time on my phone and nervously panted inside as the driver repeatedly beat traffic and then found his car being slowed down again by a chain of unmovable vehicles. After being stuck in the car for hours, we finally arrived at the airport but at the departure time.

I missed my flight. Was this a sign? Could it be that Allah was getting my attention? I was anxious, worried and afraid all at once. I stood there clueless, not knowing what Allah had in store for me.